DEDICATED
TO
MY REVERED TEACHER
LATE BIDHU BHUSAN MANNA

FRAGRANT FLOWERS FOR HOMES AND GARDENS TRADE AND INDUSTRY

S.C. Dey

ABHINAV PUBLICATIONS

abhinav publications

First published in India 1996

Publishers
Shakti Malik
Abhinav Publications
E-37 Hauz Khas
New Delhi-110016

ISBN 81-7017-335-3

Phototypeset in Platino 11pt by
Tara Chand Sons
Naraina
New Delhi

Printed at
D.K. Fine Art Press Pvt. Ltd.
Ashok Vihar
Delhi

Contents

Preface

The language of flowers is understood by one and all—it is of love, beauty and serenity. The sweet perfume of a flower tends to appeal to our senses as does a rural landscape, a fine painting, a pretty maiden or a sweet note of music. Fragrance emanates from the perfume-content of the flower in the form of volatile oil. The more the flowers are sweetly scented the more they have their economic importance. Hence their inclusion in the economic botany. Jasmine, rose and tuberose are very important commodities of cut-flower trade as well as of perfumery on account of their strong and sweet fragrance. They are good exchange earners, mainly because essential oils extracted from them find extensive popularity all over the world. In internal as well as foreign markets of fresh-flower trade also they are equally good as they fetch more prices than others. Home gardeners also cannot but lend preference to them for their elegance and perfume.

The cultural hints for the home gardeners, the agro-technique for commercial growers, the process-technology for perfumery, the descriptive botany for the identification of various species and cultivars and breeding procedures for bringing about improvements over the existing cultivars are the essential things which, one presumes, to be contained in a single compendium. Unfortunately such a useful literature on fragrant flowers had never been in existence until the present volume was published.

Till the recent past flowers were mainly grown for temples, ceremonial offerings, festive occasions and for pleasure. Today the culture of fragrant flowers has developed into a vast industry in many countries. The recent trend in this direction in our country is obviously a good sign. For the sake of rural development more emphasis has recently been laid on agro-industries. Vistas are being explored to exploit all agro-products for trade and industry. The technology for industrial use of jasmine for the production of valuable jasmine oil has been developed at Tamil Nadu Agricultural University under a scheme sponsord by the Indian Council of Agricultural Research. The National Botanical Research Institute of Lucknow has also developed new technique and apparatus for extraction of jasmine and rose oils. The Council of Scientific and Industrial Research (New Delhi) has published valuable literature—the Wealth of India, 18 volumes of which contain valuable information on raw materials and industrial products of Indian perfumery among various other things. The Central Institute of Medicinal and Aromatic Plants (Pantnagar) is also doing a lot for the development of industry based on flower-perfume. In this age of information explosion it is really difficult to collect all necessary and relevant information on a subject at one's command. In view of this the present volume has been made a compendium in which one will find all-round information on planting materials, flower production, processing technology and marketing of the products. So it will be of immense use to the teachers and students of botany and horticulture, home gardeners as well as market growers, horticultural superintending personnel and nurserymen, landscape architects and bio-aesthetic planners. The personnel attached to social forestry, the technologists of agro-horticultural research stations and public farms, the officers of horticultural development and block-level workers helping the farming communities will also find it very useful. Needless to say, the persons interested in perfumery, agro-based or synthetic, will find the book a storehouse of information including process-technology.

I am thankful to those who have extended their help in preparing the manuscript and illustrations. I am specially grateful to Sri Arun Kumar Acharya (Berhampur, Ganjam) who supplied me the information on *Kewda* distillation and to Sri V.C. Karuna (T.N. Agricultural University, Coimbatore) who supplied me some important photographs, jasmine seeds and other germplasms for originating new cultivars having essential oil.

Horticultural Arena
Jhargram, PIN 721507
1st September 1994

S.C. Dey

Introduction

Bio-aesthetic planning for improving the environment of human beings is just as imperative. The surrounding laden with flower-perfume has its bearing on making the environment beautiful and refreshing the minds of those living in the vicinity.

In view of the rapid development of rural economy the technology for villages has become a cry. This is due to the information-gap that urges the transfer of technology to the rural folk. As the library facilities are inadequate for the disadvantaged it is difficult to collect information on technology lying disorganized in numerous journals and research papers. On account of the scarcity of published information on Indian trade and industry that can at least be a guideline to potential traders and entrepreneurs they have to collect much of the necessary information through correspondence and personal contacts with the manufacturers, technologists and government departments. With a view to filling up that gap the book has been designed to make it a storehouse of information on agro-products, raw materials, process-technology and marketing. Flowers being the agro-products for trading and raw materials of perfume industry the information as to the appropriate cultivars and the agro-technique involved for their commercial production are of prime importance. They have been classified and put into different chapters. The descriptive botany (morphology), classification (taxonomy), different names (local or popular) and the distribution of cultivars are the essentials that help to identify the plants correctly. All these have been incorporated in Chapter 1 — BOTANY.

The cultural methods or agro-technique is an important

thing in which a grower must be well versed for optimum production of flower crops. The propagation of planting materials for commercial planting is usually entrusted to the nurserymen as it demands professional skill as well as the source of certified and healthy germplasms. Still a part of Chapter 2 has been devoted to plant propagation. For certain types of materials growers may have to depend on foreign sources. The tuberose bulb is one of such materials in which case bulb growing and raising flower crop are usually two different industries in certain countries. Due attention is paid to illustrate the difference in Chapter 2 — HORTICULTURE.

The information relating to cut-flower trade, such as post-harvest handling, packaging, transporting to trans-continental markets, prolonging the life of cut flowers etc. has been dealt with in Chapter 3 — CUT-FLOWER TRADE.

The different processes involved in the extraction of essential oils, the marketing of different types of floral products—from crude extracts to finished floral compounds—have been presented in Chapter 4 — ESSENTIAL OIL INDUSTRY.

The glossary of technical terms, the directory containing names of relevant government departments, research stations and firms (for inputs), and exhaustive bibliographical references and indices separately for cultivars and general matters with cross-references have been appended.

It is a universally acknowledged fact that good illustrations not only enhance aesthetics but also reinforce the text. With a view to making the work accomplished and more interesting to the readers endeavours have been made to illustrate fully with relevant photographs and figures.

List of Illustrations

Line Drawings

1

Botany

This chapter deals with the description of plants which facilitates identification of species or cultivars. The emphasis is laid on the characteristics which differentiate one species from its closely related ones. Latin binomials for the botanical names and English vernacular names have been used here. Local names used in different parts of the country are given in the next chapter—HORTICULTURE. Natural distribution of the species has also been mentioned here. All these together will help identify the species correctly.

TREES

Albizzia lebbek, Benth.

Family: Leguminosae

Eng. vernac: East Indian Walnut

A tree with an umbrella-shaped crown, height 14-18 m, bark yellowish. *Leaves* feathery, leaflets 3-9 pairs, 2-3 cm long, obliquely elliptic. *Flowers* greenish white in tassel-like heads, fragrant; the central flo-

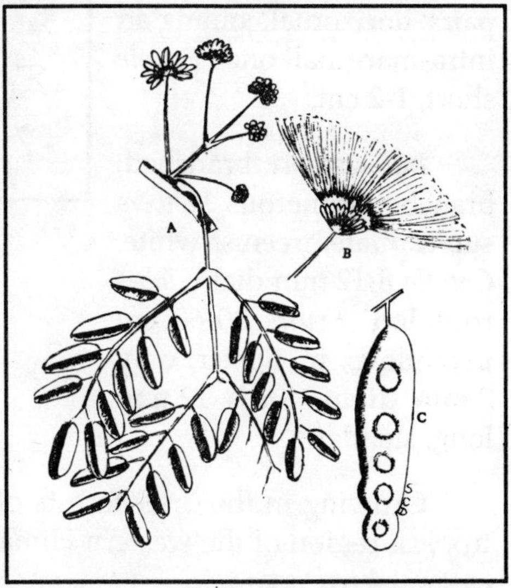

ALBIZZIA LEBBEK

A. Portion of a Branch with inflorescence B. Head with Flowers C. Pod

ret differing in shape from the rest. *Petals* rudimentary but conspicuous only in the central floret. *Stamen* numerous with long thin filaments giving the flower head a powder puff-like appearance. *Pods* flat and long (15-25 cm), straw colour, similar to that of the bark.

Extensively grown in the gardens of India. Wild in the sub-Himalayan tract, Bengal, Chota Nagpur and the Andamans.

Alstonia scholaris R. Br.
Family: Apocynaceae
Eng. vernac. name: Devil's tree

An evergreen tree, 14-30 m; trunk tall branches whorled; latex white. *Leaves* 4-8, usually 7, width 10-15 cm very coriaceous, whitish beneath; *Nerves* 30-60 pairs, horizontal, joining an intra-marginal one. *Petiole* short, 1-2 cm.

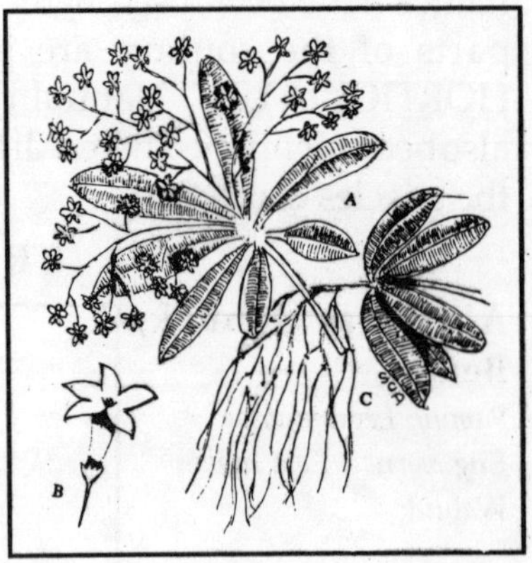

ALSTONIA SCHOLARIS
A. Shoot with inflorescence
B. Flower
C. Bunch of long pods

Inflorescence branched; branches numerous. *Flowers* sub-capitate, greenish white. *Corolla* 8-12 mm diam; *lobes* rounded. *Fruits* 30-60 cm pendulous, in cluster, only 3 mm diam. *Seeds* 12 mm long, slender.

Growing in the drier forests of India and in the sub-tropical region of the western Himalaya from the Yamuna eastward to Assam.

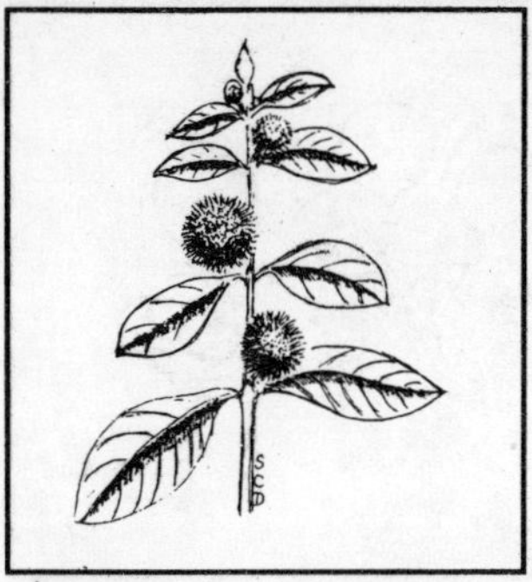

ANTHOCEPHALUS INDICUS

Anthocephalus indicus, A. Rich (Syn. *A. cadamba*)

Family: Rubiaceae

Popular name: Kadamba

Tall tree, growing to a height of 15-20 m with a clean straight cylindrical stem and horizontal branches. *Leaves* large, 15-20 cm opposite. *Flowers* small, greenish yellow, arranged on spherical heads, 5-8 cm in diam, fragrant. *Fruit* globose, 3-5 cm wide, first green then brownish.

Growing in sub-Himalayan tracts from Nepal eastwards to Burma, and in the Southern and Western Ghats.

Citrus aurantium, Linn.

Family: Rutaceae

Eng vernac: Orange, sour orange

A medium size much branched thorny tree with rounded top. *Leaves* dark green, medium sized, 7-10 cm more or less acuminate at the tip. *Petiole* broadly winged. Flowers medium sized, axillary, single or clustered. *Petals* 5, white on both sides, very fragrant. *Stamens* 20-24. Ovary globular. *Fruits* round mostly rough and warty, orange (in colour) when ripe, size various. *Pulp* strongly acid, membranous with a bitter taste, segments 10-12. *Rind* aromatic, bitter and pungent.

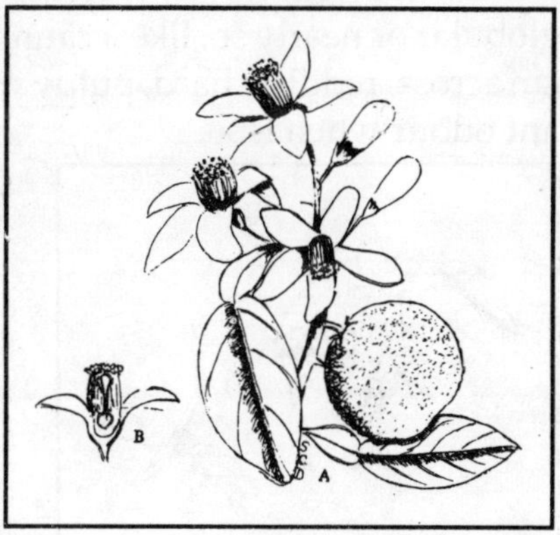

CITRUS AURANTIUM

A. Branch with Fruit, Flowers and Buds

B. Flower, Vertical Section

Native of Northern India, distributed all over the world.

Coroupita guianensis, Auble

Family: Lecythidaceae

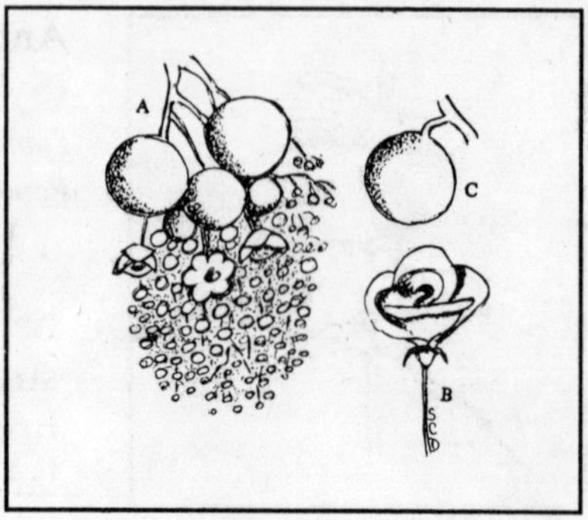

COROUPITA GUIANENSIS
A. Inflorescence with Fruits, Flowers and Buds
B. Flower C. Fruit

A tall soft-wooded tree, about 15-20 m high with a large spreading crown, *Leaves* alternate, oblong-obovate with rounded teeth, 12-16 cm long; deciduous, dropping twice or thrice a year. *Flowers* about 8 cm across, fragrant with concave petals, yellow and red tinged on the exterior and crimson-lilac within, very showy, in racemes 75 cm to 1 m long. *Fruits* globular or nearly so, like a cannon ball of olden days, 15-20 cm across, reddish, hard, pulpy within and with an unpleasant odour when ripe.

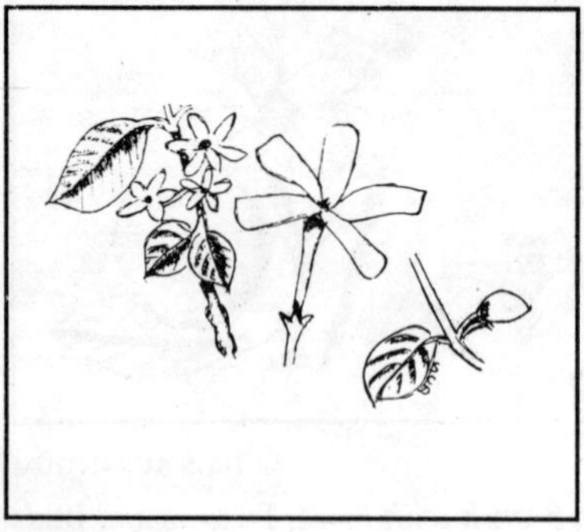

GARDENIA LATIFOLIA
A. Branch with Flower
B. Flower
C. Fruit

Gardenia latifolia, Ait

Family: Rubiaceae

A small tree with woody branchlets as thick as the small finger, sometimes epiphytic. *Leaves* greenish, opposite, large, broad and elliptic, 10-25 cm long. *Nerves* about 12 pairs, stipules large, tumid, connate, often split and toothed. *Flowers* solitary, white, changing to yellow, fragrant, calyx limb campanulate; segments 5-9 unequal, recurved, corolla-tube 5-8 cm; limb 5-12 cm diam; lobes 5-9. *Fruit* globose, 25-50 mm diam, pubescent edible, seeds numerous.

Growing in the dry forests of Western, Central and South-western India, distributed all over the world.

Madhuca indica (Syn. *Bassia latifolia*, Roxb)

Family: Sapotaceae

Eng vernac: Moa-tree

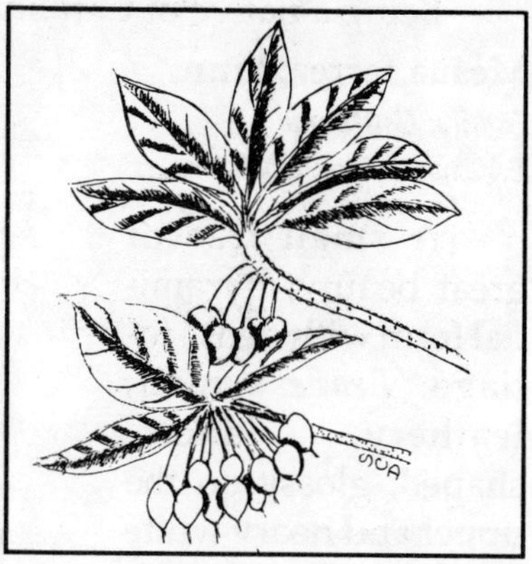

MADHUCA INDICA
Branches with Bead-like Flowers

A tree, 17m with a large head. *Leaves* 13 x 8 cm varying in size and form round-obovate to broad lanceolate, acute. *Flowers* 2 cm, yellowish white, tube fleshy, *lobes* 7-14 short, erect. *Stamens* usually 24-26; anthers hairy, acuminate. *Berry* 3-5 cm, ovoid 1-4 seeded.

Madhuca longifolia, Linn.

Leaves lanceolate narrowed at both ends, glabrescent, distinctly nerved. *Corolla* 2 cm, lobes usually 6, scarcely one third the length of the tube. Other aspects being same as *M. indica.*

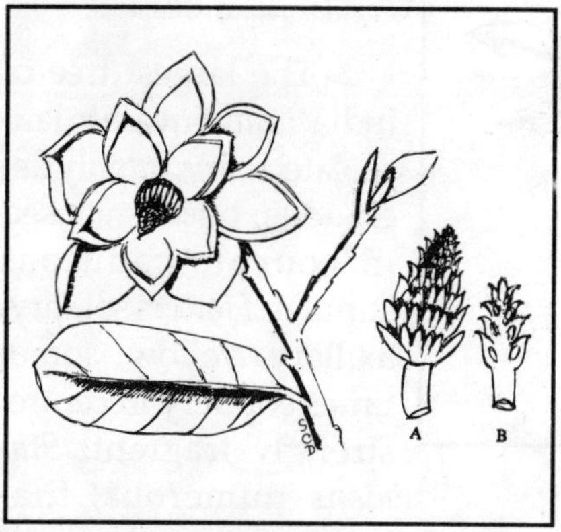

MAGNOLIA GANDIFLORA
A. Stamens and Carpels B. Carpels

Magnolia grandiflora, Linn.

Family: Magnoliaceae

Eng. vernac: Bull Bay

A handsome evergreen small tree with pyramidal form, widely cultivated in Indian gardens, found up to an altitude of 2000 m in the Himalayas. *Leaves* large, firm, laurel-like, obovate-oblong, glossy above, pubescent and reddish brown beneath. *Flowers* cup-shaped, 15-20 cm diam, yellowish white to white. *Fruit* ovoid, tomentose. *Seeds* bright red (size—tamarind stone) ripen in August.

Being a native of Carolina.

Mesua ferrea, Linn.

Family: Guttiferae

E.V. name: Iron wood tree

MESUA FERREA

Branch with Flowers and Fruit

A small tree of great beauty, pyramidal form with dense foliage. *Leaves* small, leathery, lancet-shaped, glossy on the upper and hoary white on the lower surface. *Flowers* large, white, 4-petalled, delightfully fragrant. *Fruit* dehiscent, 1-celled, opening by 4 valves.

Commonly found in Assam and lower Bengal.

BRANCH OF MICHELIA CHAMPACA

A. Stamens and Carpels

B. Fruits C. Seeds

Michelia champaca, Linn.

Family: Magnoliaceae

Popular name: Champak

The largest tree of India. *Leaves* ovate to lanceolate, hairy, mainly deciduous; buds enclosed in connate caducous stipules. *Flowers* solitary, axillary, yellow, sometimes coppery in centre, strongly fragrant. *Stamens* numerous, filaments flat, anthers adnate and introrse. *Carpels* many free ripening to ovoid woody fruits. *Seeds* dark brown, angular with bright pink fleshy aril.

Being a native of Peninsular India.

M. alba (Syn. *M. longifolia*) Macbr.

Popular name: Swet champa

Large tree. *Leaves* ovate not deciduous, glabrous, buds enclosed in connate caducous stipules. *Flowers* solitary, axillary, white, fragrant. *Carpels* many free ripening to malformed woody fruits.

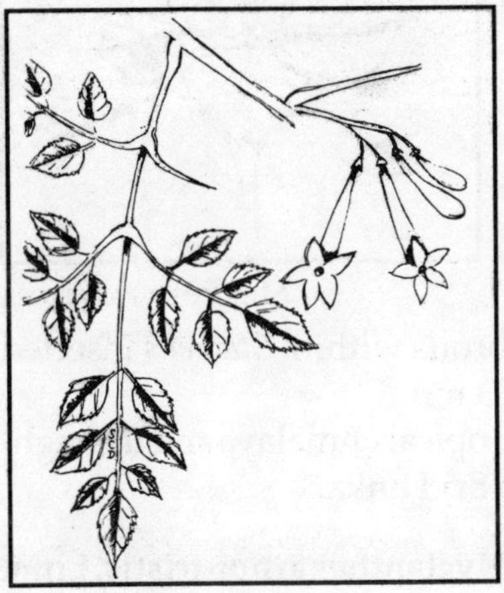

MILLINGTONIA HORTENSIS

Millingtonia hortensis, Linn.

Family: Bignoniaceae

Eng vernac: Indian cork tree

Trees growing in a straight elongated pyramidal form up to 25 m high. *Leaves* compound, ornamental, resembling those of *Neem* (*Azadirachta indica*); leaflets oval to oval-lanceolate, margins dentate. *Flowers* in terminal panicles, pendulous, white, fragrant. *Fruit* capsule, slender; seeds many, flat winged.

Being indigenous to Burma and Malay Archipelago. Growing in many Indian forests. Found in gardens and avenues throughout India.

Mimusops elengi, Linn.

Family: Sapotaceae

Eng. vernac: Bulletwood tree

An elegant evergreen tree with round and compact crown. *Leaves* elliptic and short-acuminate (7-9 cm long) rhomboid at the base. *Corolla-lobes* about 6, narrow lanceolate. *Stamens* 8, *Fruit* 2 cm, ovoid, 1 or 2 seeded, yellow, edible.

MIMUSOPS ELENGI

Shoots with fruits, flowers and buds

Native of East Indies. Growing in parks, gardens and avenues.

Mitragyna parviflora, korth.
(Syns. Stephegyne parviflora, Nauclea parviflora, Willd.)

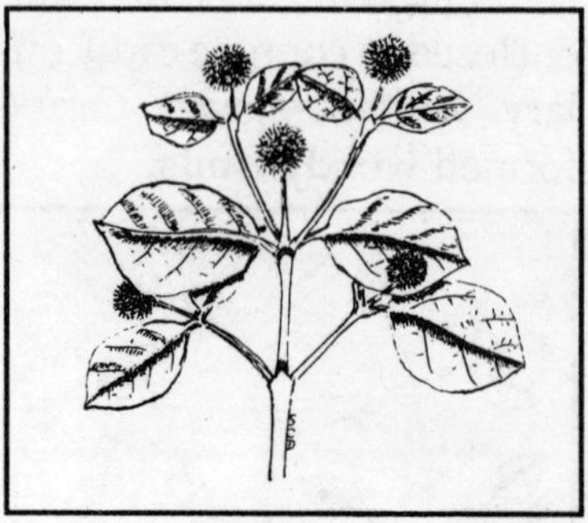

MITRAGYNA PARVIFLORA

A small or large tree, glabrous or pubescent. *Leaves* extremely variable in size and shape, deciduous, 5-15 cm, petiole short; stipules obovate. *Heads* about 2-3 cm diam, with two linear-oblong leaves at the base. *Corolla* glabrous within. *Stamens* inserted in the tube. *Capsules* (fruits) 33 mm.

Growing in dry forest of tropical Himalaya and throughout the drier parts of India to Sri Lanka.

Nyctanthes arbor-tristis, Linn.
Family: Oleaceae
Eng. vernac: Night jasmine, Coral jasmine and Tree of sadness

NYCTANTHES ARBOR-TRISTIS
A. Inflorescence
B. Flower
C. Fruit

A hardy large shrub or small tree with large broad leaves, branchlets quadrangular. *Leaves* obovate, acuminate, rough and glabrous above, densely pubescent beneath. *Flowers* small in trichotomous cymes; corolla fragrant, white, 4-8 lobes with the coral orange tube. *Capsules* flattened, 2-celled with one seed in each.

Growing in the forest of central India. Cultivated throughout India and both hemispheres.

Plumeria

Family: Apocynaceae
Eng. vernac: Frangipani,
Temple tree, Pagoda tree, etc.

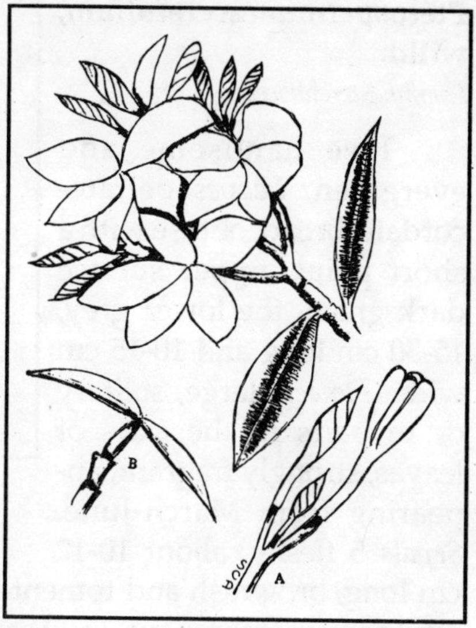

FLOWERING SHOOT OF PLUMERIA
A. Flower and Buds
B. Fruits

Trees small with very thick branches, fleshy bark and spreading heads. *Leaves* elongated, large; nerves parallel, spreading from a strong mid-rib. *Flowers* large in terminal 2-3 chotomous cymes; petals 5, connate in a salver shaped corolla; lobes overlapping. *Stamens* 5, adnate near base of the tube; anthers obtuse. *Carpels* 2, distinct; ovule many; style short, enclosed in the tube. *Fruit* of 2 linear-oblong or ellipsoid follicles; seeds winged.

P. acutifolia, Poir.

Trees deciduous. *Leaves* broadly lanceolate with long tapering ends, light green in colour. *Flowers* creamy white with yellow centre, outside pinkish, strongly fragrant. *Fruits* twine follicle (horn-like).

P. alba, Ait.

Trees evergreen or partly deciduous. *Leaves* oblanceolate or elliptic, hairy below, 15-20 cm or more long, dark green in colour. *Flowers* large, white with yellow centre, strongly and deliciously fragrant. *Fruits* twine follicle (horn-like).

P. rubra, Linn.

A small tree. *Flowers* red, pink or purple with rich yellow centre. Known as 'Lal champa' in Marathi.

Pterospermum acerefolium, willd.
Family: Sterculiaceae

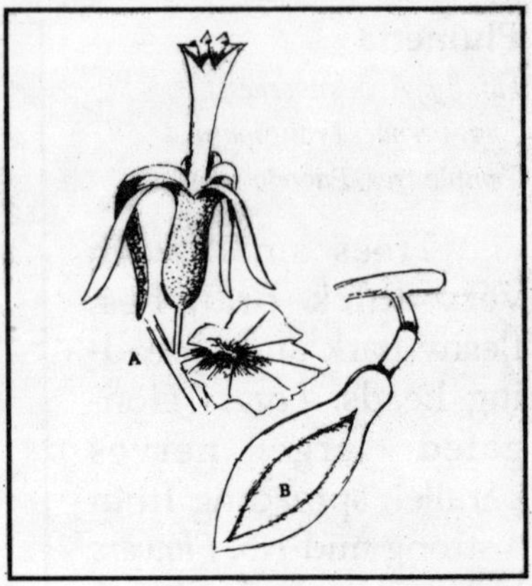

PTEROSPERMUM ACEREFOLIUM
A. Flower
B. Fruit

Tree handsome and evergreen. *Leaves* peltate-cordate, broad, obtuse with a short point, upper surface dark green, the lower grey, 15-30 cm long and 10-15 cm wide. *Flowers* large, solitary or in pairs in the axils of leaves, strongly fragrant, appearing from March-June. *Sepals* 5 fleshy, about 10-12 cm long, brownish and tomentose on the outside. *Petals* 5, white and membranous. *Fruit* capsule 10-14 cm long, oblong 5 angled, covered with a dense coating of woody hairs; seeds brown, compressed with large membranous terminal wings.

A native of the Himalayas, Assam and Burma.

SHRUBS

Cestrum nocturnum, Linn.
Family: Solanaceae
E.V. name: Night blooming jasmine

A perfect shrub, 1-1.5 m in height; branches greenish, very slender, glabrous. *Leaves* prominently acuminate. *Flowers* greenish white; corolla lobes ovate and blunt; filaments denticulate. *Berry* ovoid-oblong.

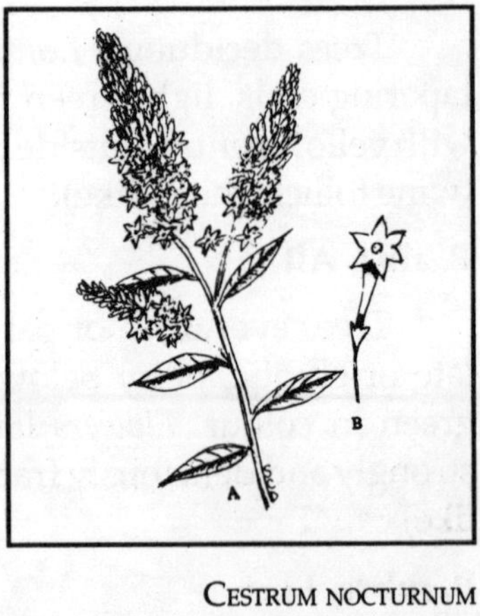

CESTRUM NOCTURNUM
A. Branch with Inflorescence
B. Flower

Gardenia
Family: Rubiaceae
Eng vernac: Gardenia, Cape jasmine etc.

Named in honour of Dr. Alexander Garden, an 18th century botanist from South Carolina. A genus of evergreen shrub (from tropical Asia and tropical South Africa) noted for its fragrant flowers. Having deliciously scented flowers. Growing in gardens in all parts of the country.

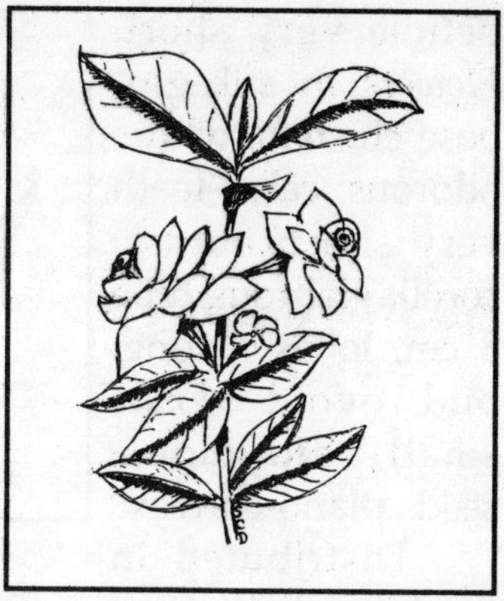

GARDENIA
Branch with Flowers and Buds

G. florida, Linn.
(Syn. G. jasminoides, Ellis)

Large shrubs or small trees. *Leaves* large, elliptic-ovate, thick, glossy. *Flowers* solitary, 7 cm across, white, turning yellowish on staling, double, not symmetrical. *Fruit* ovoid 3-4 cm long, orange in colour, fruit setting rare in India.

G. fortunei

A dwarf version of *G. florida*; plant bushy, foliage more glossy and darker than the former. *Flowers* fully double and rose-like but less floriferous.

Having a dwarf cultivar named 'Radicans', very dwarf; leaves small; flowers small, well formed with delicious scent.

G. kirkii

Flowers star-shaped, single; *leaves* dark green.

G. veitchii

A winter flowering variety having fine flowers.

Ixora parviflora, Vahl
Family: Rubiaceae

An evergreen shrub or small tree. *Leaves* 10-15 x 5-7 cm,

petiole very short. *Flowers* in sub-globose clusters, white, odorous; calyx-teeth very short, obtuse; corolla glabrous, tube 8 cm, lobes oblong, bud ovoid. *Fruit* small, didymous, seeds plano-convex.

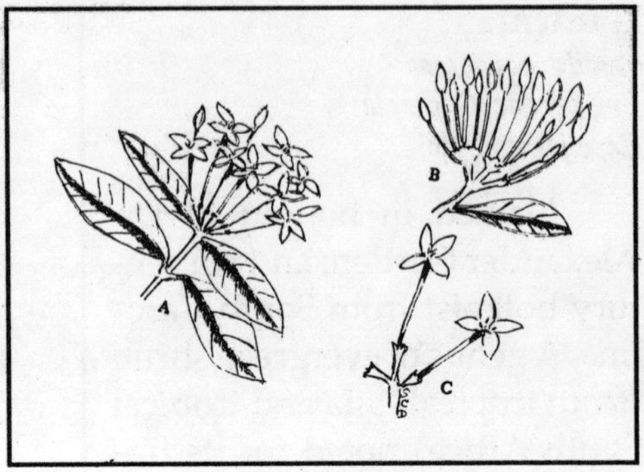

IXORA PARVIFLORA
A. Branch with Inflorescence
B. Buds C. Flowers

Distributed in the hilly districts of West Bengal, Bihar and in Western Peninsula, from the Satpura range southwards.

Jasminum officinale, Linn.

Family: Oleaceae

A long slender grower requiring support. *Leaves* opposite, imparipinnately compound with 3-7 leaflets; terminal leaflet larger than the laterals, glossy. *Inflorescence* terminal cymes. *Flowers* white with 4-7 lobes, fragrant. *Fruit* globose, black when ripe.

A native of Persia or Kashmir growing at an altitude of 1000-3000 m, cultivated in gardens throughout the world.

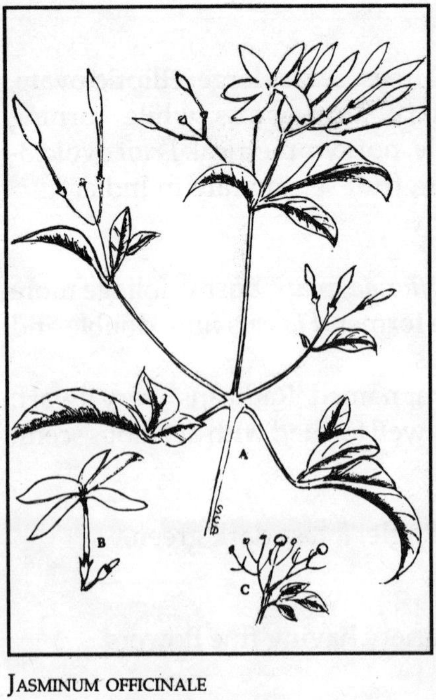

JASMINUM OFFICINALE
A. Branch with Inflorescence
B. Flower and Bud C. Twig with Fruits

J. grandiflorum, Linn.
Eng. vernac: Royal jasmine, Catalonian jasmine, Italian jasmine, Spanish jasmine, etc.

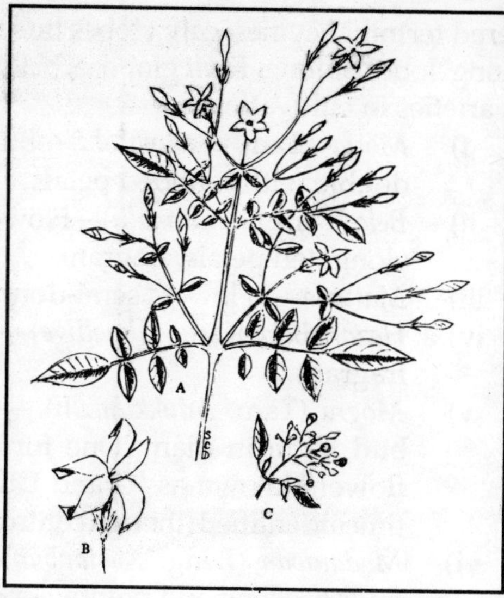

JASMINUM GRANDIFLORUM
A. Flowering Branch
B. Flower
C. Twig with Fruits

A large climbing shrub, branches furrowed. *Leaves* opposite, imparipinnately compound; leaflets 7-11, terminal leaflet larger than the lateral.

Inflorescence long terminal cymes. *Flowers* white often tinged with mauve on the outside, deliciously fragrant. *Fruit* globose, black when ripe.

Believed to be a native of N.W. Himalaya and introduced into Europe from India through Spanish navigators. Extensively grown all over India. Cultivars having double flowers also found in gardens.

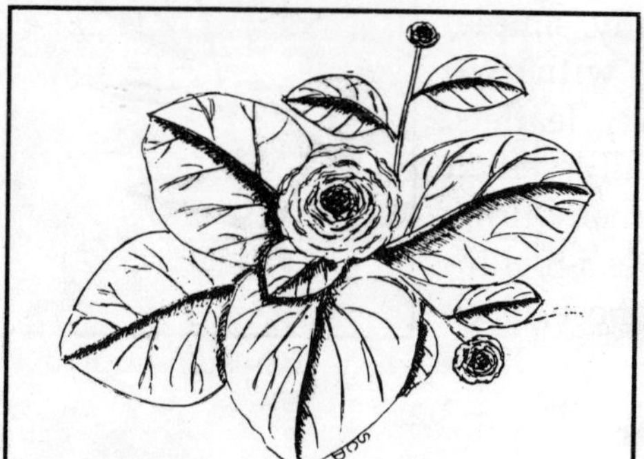

JASMINUM SAMBAC

J. sambac, Linn.
Eng. vernac: Arabian jasmine, Tuscan jasmine etc.

A sub-erect shrub cultivated in tropical and subtropical climates. *Leaves* opposite or sometimes ternate (ternate-leaved specimen named as *J. trifoliatum,* Hort), firm in texture, glossy, glabrous or nearly so. *Flowers* white or creamy but turning purplish on staling, strongly fragrant, solitary or in 3-flowered terminal cymes; calyx lobes linear; corolla tube 15 mm long, lobes oblong. *Fruit* globose, black when ripe. Different varieties in cultivation

i) *Motia* (Tam. *Virupakshi*)—Buds globular; flowers double with rounded petals.
ii) *Bela* (Tam. *Gundumalli*)—Flowers double, white with elongated petals, fragrant.
iii) *Maturia* — Flowers semi-double, white, fragrant.
iv) *Hazara Bela* (Kan. *Sujimallige*)—Flowers single, white, fragrant.
v) *Mogra* (Tam. *Adukkumalli*) — Flowers full double; bud 3 cm in diam. One form with creamy white flowers known as 'Grand Duke of Tascany' sometimes identified (though controversial) as *J. trifoliatum*.
vi) *Madanwan* (Beng. *Madanban*) — Unlike others its buds are long and pointed opening of which is sudden and startling.

J. auriculatum, Vahl

Popular name: Juhi

A scandent, pubescent shrub found in the Deccan Peninsula and cultivated in gardens throughout India. *Leaves* apparently simple, but mostly trifoliate with two minute or rudimentary leaflets. *Flowers* white, delightfully scented borne in compound many-flowered cymes; corolla lobes 5-8, elliptic. *Carpels* solitary, globose, black when ripe.

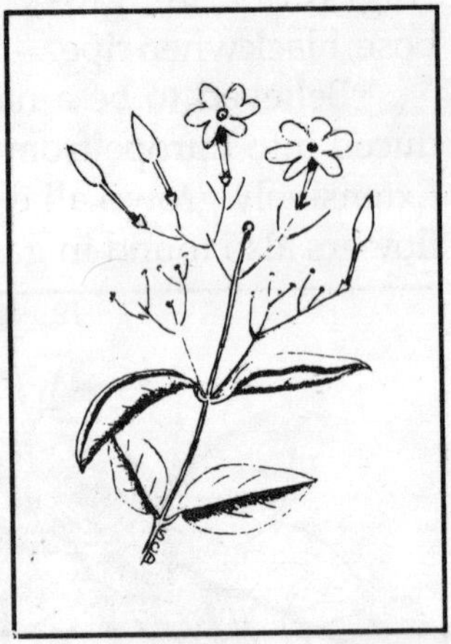

JASMINUM AURICULATUM

Multiwhorled cultivar

A double-flowered form resembling more a *J. sambac* than *J. auriculatum*.

Popular name: Double juhi

A climbing shrub growing in the gardens of India.

Leaves opposite, apparently simple. *Flowers* white, double with three whorls of corolla lobes, strongly fragrant.

Lawsonia inermis, Linn (Syn. *L. alba,* Lam)

Family: Lythraceae

Eng. Vernac: Egyptian Privet

A glabrous thickly branched shrub or small tree. *Leaves* opposite, sub-sessile, elliptic entire, acute or obtuse. *Flowers* numerous, small, white or light pink, fragrant in large terminal panicled cymes. *Capsule* (Fruit) about size of a pea with numerous pyramidal smooth seeds.

Growing as an economic plant in India, Egypt, Sudan, Persia, Madagascar, Pakistan and Australia.

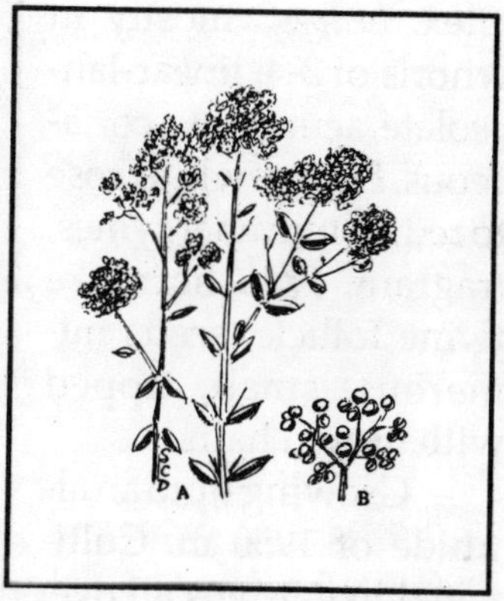

LAWSONIA INERME

A. Branches with Inflorescence

B. Fruits

Murraya paniculata (Syn. *M. exotica,* Linn)

Family: Rutaceae

Eng. Vernac.: Orange jasmine

Shrubs or small trees. *Leaves* imparipinnate. *Leaflets* 3-9, ovate, gland dotted. *Flowers* in corymbose cymes, white, fragrant; petals 5, imbricate, free. *Stamens* 10. *Berries* ovoid, red or deep orange when ripe, 1-2 seeded.

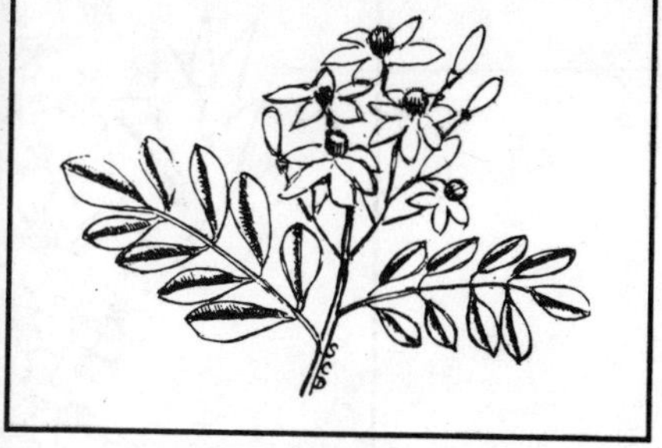

MURRAYA PANICULATA

Nerium indicum Mill (Syn. *N. odorum*, Soland)

Family: Apocynaceae

Eng. Vernac: Indian oleander, sweet scented oleander, etc.

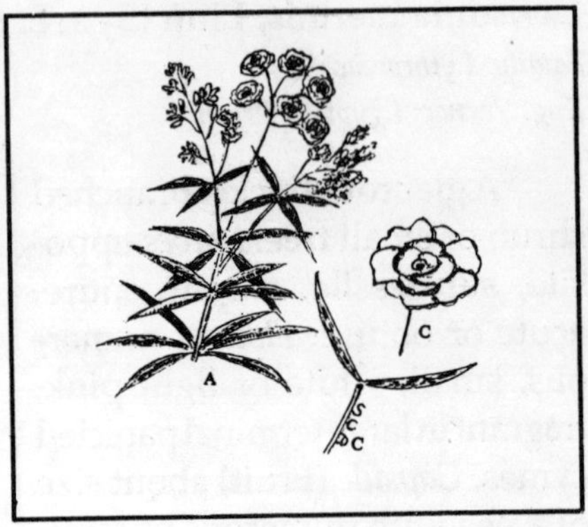

NERIUM

A. Branch with Inflorescence

B. Flower C. Fruits

Evergreen shrubs with cane-like slender flexible stems with milky latex. *Leaves* mostly in whorls of 3-4, linear-lanceolate, acuminate, coriaceous. *Flowers* white, rose to red, in terminal cymes, fragrant. *Fruit* horn-like twine follicle; seeds numerous, small, tipped with brown hairs.

Growing upto an altitude of 1950 m. Cultivated in gardens all over the world

Pandanus odoratissimus, Linn.

Family: Pandanaceae

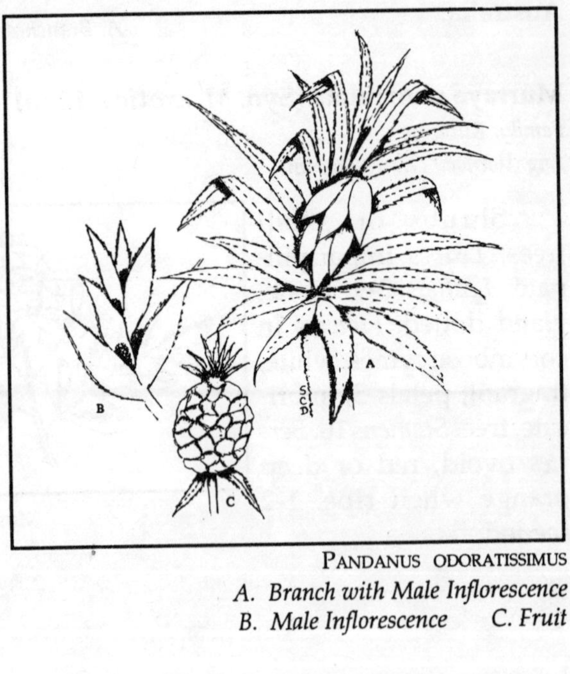

PANDANUS ODORATISSIMUS

A. Branch with Male Inflorescence

B. Male Inflorescence C. Fruit

A densely branched shrub rarely erect. *Stems* upto 6 m high and supported by stilt roots extending towards water. *Leaves* 1-1.5 m long, glaucous green, ensiform, acuminate, coriaceous with sharp spines on margins and on the mid ribs. *Flowers* male spadix 25-50 cm long with numerous subsessile cylindric spikes enclosed in long greenish white fragrant caudate acuminate spathes; female spadix solitary 5 cm in diam. *Fruit* oblong or globose, 15-25 cm in diam, yellow or red.

In India growing along the coast and in Andaman islands. On the shore growing in long stretches of impregnable vegetation above the high watermark. Owing to wide adaptability is found growing along the saline, brackish and fresh-water courses.

Rosa centifolia, Linn.

Family: Rosaceae

Eng. Vernac: Cabbage rose

Closely related to *Rosa gallica*. An upright shrub. *Stems* densely covered with shorter prickles. *Leaves* compound, leaflets usually 5, pubescent on both sides or only dorsally. *Flowers* pink, double on long and slender pedicels, fragrant; calyx persistent. *Fruit* bony achenes.

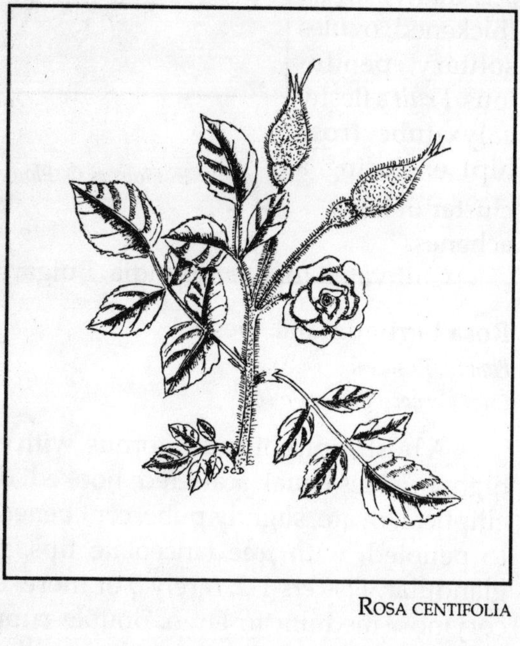

ROSA CENTIFOLIA

Cultivated in fields for oil extraction in a number of countries.

Rosa damascena, Mill.

Family: Rosaceae

Eng. Vernac.: Damask rose

A small, erect shrub, prickly. *Leaves* pinnately 7 foliate; leaflets serrate; stipules adnate. *Flowers* terminal, corymbose, pink, fragrant; sepals 5, petals many. *Stamens* many; *carpels* many; *stigma* thickened; ovules solitary, pendulous. *Fruit* a fleshy calyx-tube (rose hip) enclosing a cluster of bony achenes.

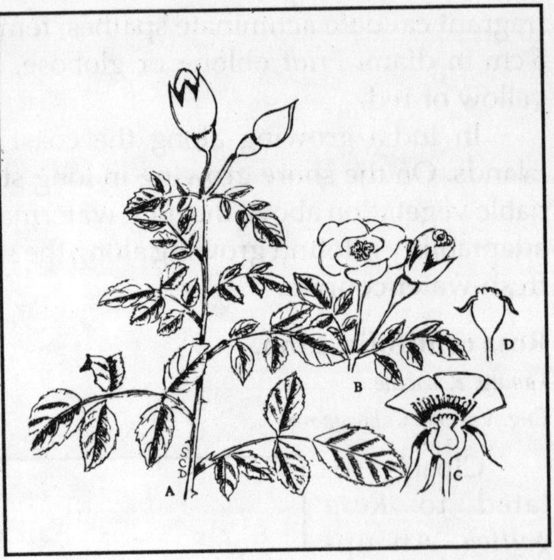

ROSA DAMASCENA

A. Branch with Buds

B. Flowers C. Flower, Vertical Sec D. Fruit

Cultivated for *attar* in India, Bulgaria, France etc.

Rosa borbouniana, Desp.

Family: Rosaceae

Eng. Vernac.: Edward rose

A bush, upright and vigorous, with erect shoots 1½-2 m high; prickles equal, scattered, hooked, dilated. *Leaflets* 5-7, elliptical, ovate, slightly pubescent beneath; stipules adnate to petioled, with free lanceolate tips; margins pectinate, glandular. *Flowers* 1-2, rarely 5 or more, usually in terminal corymbs, medium to large, double cupped; colour white, pink or red; pendundcle long thick with glandular bristles;

sepals leafy; petals soft, velvety, fragrant with rose scent.

Originated as a natural hybrid of the Damask and China roses at the end of the 18th century in the Isles of Bourbon, now known as 'Island of Reunion' in the Indian Ocean. Cultivated commercially both in northern and southern India for perfume production.

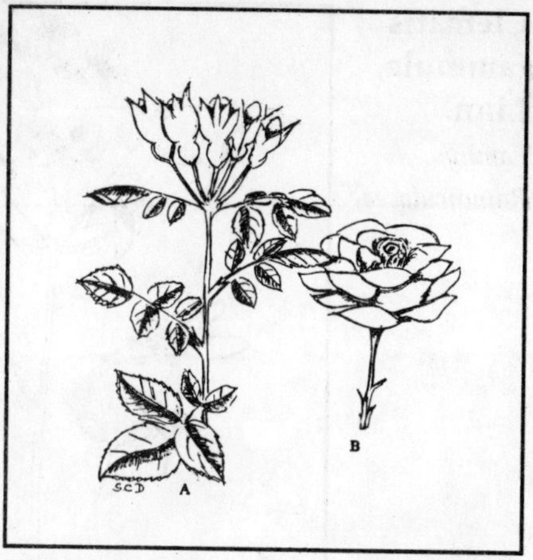

EDWARD ROSE
A. Flowering Branch B. Flower

CLIMBERS

Artabotrys odoratissimus R. Br.
(Syn. Uvaria odoratissimus)
Family: Annonaceae

A climbing shrub. *Leaves* shining glabrous. *Flowers* solitary on woody hooked recurved penduncular branches with fruity fragrance. *Petals* 6, valvate, in two series with connivent concave bases, yellowish green. *Stamens* numerous. *Carpels* many, free. *Fruit* many from free carpels of a flower.

Growing in gardens throughout Eastern India.

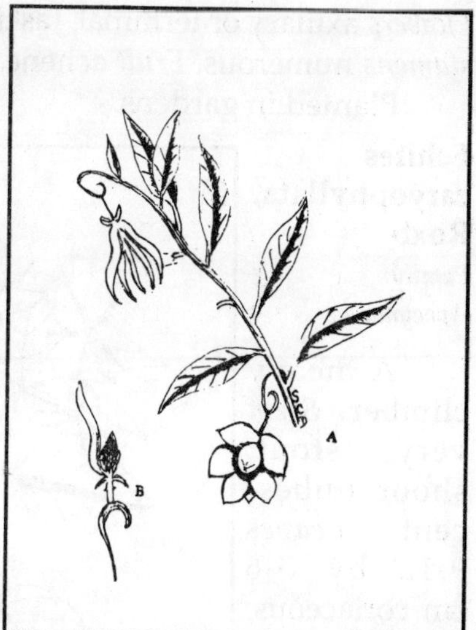

ARTABOTRYS ODORATISSIMUS
A. Branch with a Flower and Fruits
B. Stamens and Carpels

Clematis fammula, Linn.
Family: Ranunculaceae

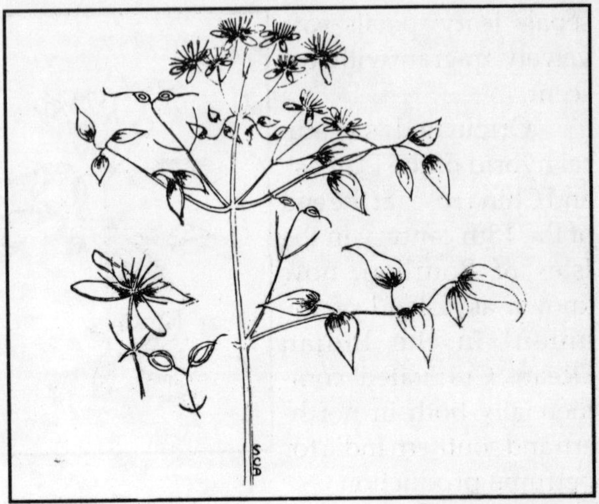

CLEMATIS FAMMULA

A climbing undershrub. *Leaves* opposite, compound; petiole sometimes twining but not produced as a tendril. *Flowers* axillary or terminal, fascicled or paniculate. *Petals* 4, *stamens* numerous. *Fruit* achenes with the style persistent.

Planted in gardens.

Echites caryophyllata, Roxb
Family: Apocynaceae

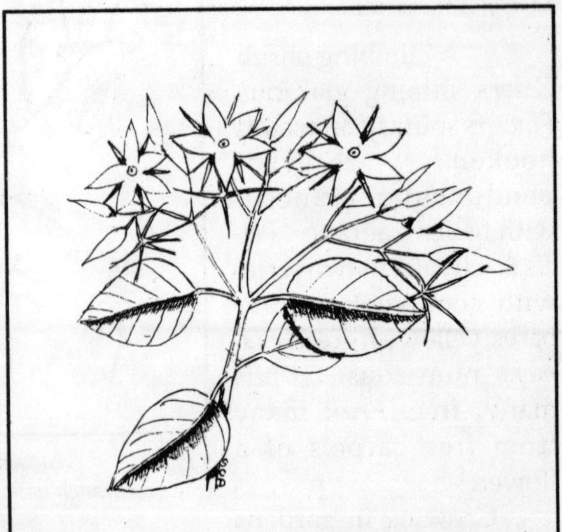

ECHITES CARYOPHYLLATA

A heavy climber. *Stem* very stout; shoot pubescent. *Leaves* 9-12 by 5-6 cm, coriaceous; nerves strong, beneath and all running towards the apex; petiole 6-12 mm. *Inflorescence* terminal, latex white; corolla-tube cylindric, limb 4 cm diam. *Ovary* pubescent; style slender. *Fruit* stout nearly 12 mm diam; seeds oval-oblong, 12 mm long, flat.

Growing in lower Bengal and Deccan Peninsula.

Passiflora caerulea, Linn.

Family: Passifloraceae

Eng. vernac.: Passion flower

A climbing shrub with simple tendrils. *Leaves* palmately lobed, stipules leafy. *Flowers* solitary, sepals 5, connate in a fleshy calyx-tube; petals 5, inserted on calyx-throat, with corona of slender filaments within the corolla, springing from throat of calyx; anthers oblong, dorsifixed. *Carpels* 3, connate in a one-celled ovary; ovules numerous; *stigmas* reniform, capitate. *Fruit* a fleshy berry; seeds many.

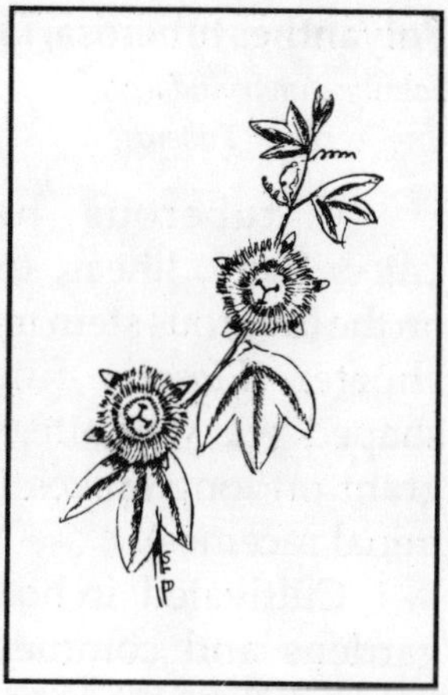

PASSION FLOWER

Quisqualis indica, Linn.

Family: Combretaceae

Eng. vernac.: Rangoon creeper

A large climbing shrub. *Leaves* opposite, oblong or obovate, acuminate, entire. *Flowers* in short axillary or terminal pendulous racemes, white changing to light red, fragrant. *Petals* 5, small, corolla tube slender and long. *Stamens* 10, short. *Carpel* solitary, inferior, style filiform, sub-adnate to calyx tube. *Fruits* 5 angled.

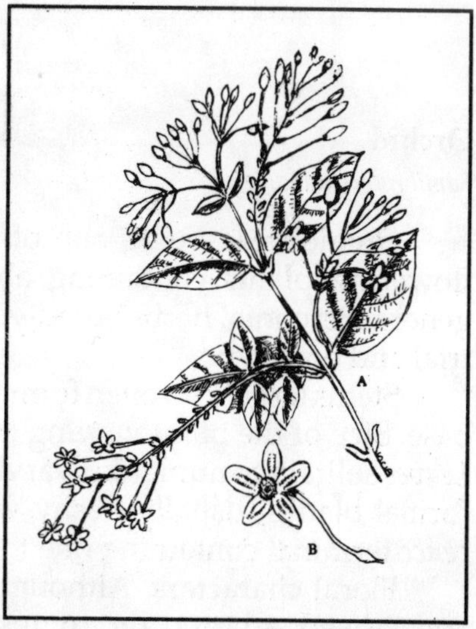

QUISQUALIS INDICA
A. Branch with Inflorescence
B. Flower

Probably indigenous, both in tropical Africa and tropical Indo-Malayan regions. Cultivated in gardens throughout India, upto the altitude of 300 m.

BULBOUS PLANTS

Polyanthes tuberosa, Linn.

Family: Amaryllidaceae

Eng. vernac.: Tuberose

A tuberous herb. *Leaves* basal, linear, those on the tuberous stem much shorter. *Flowers* funnel shaped waxy, white, fragrant on long spikes (terminal racemes).

Cultivated in homes, gardens and commercial fields all over the world.

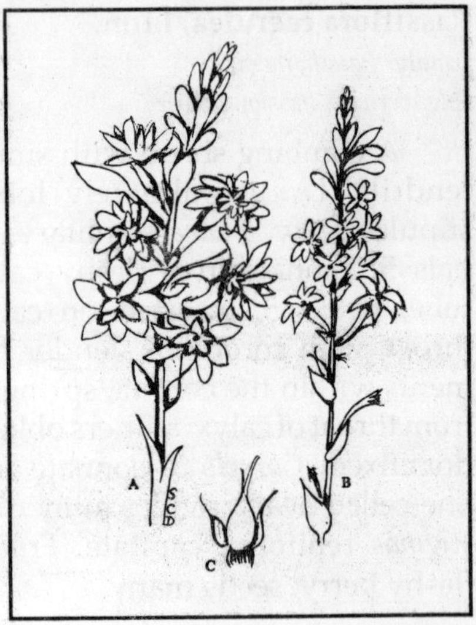

TUBEROSE
A. Spike with Double Flowers
B. Spike with Single Flowers
C. Bulb

Orchid

Family: Orchidaceae

Orchidaceae being one of the largest families of the flowering plants containing about 30,000 species in 800 genera. Perennial herbs broadly grouped into two — terrestrial and epiphytic.

Stems largely swollen forming bulb-like structure at the base. Size of the plant varying from 6 mm to 6 m in height. *Leaves* solitary to numerous varying from sheathing bracts to formal blades, usually fleshy with parallel veins. *Inflorescence* terminal containing one to many flowers.

Floral characters: Although a monocot having highly specialised adaptation to insect pollination. Extreme specialisation lying in that its lip simulating a queen bee attracting male bees for obvious reasons other than collecting honey.

Perianth consisting of six parts—three sepals and three petals arising from the top of the ovary. *Petals* 3, one of them modified into 'lip'; lips being larger and more striking than the other petals, varying in form pouch-shaped or flat to curiously lobed and fringed or spurred, often strikingly coloured than the other petals as in most pansies.

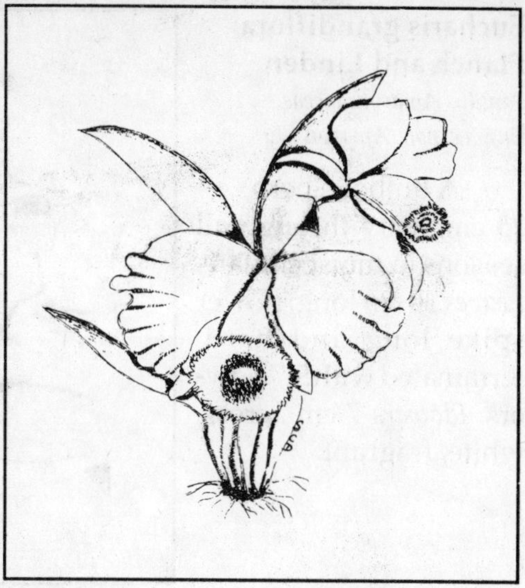

ORCHID (CATTLEYA)

Hedychium coronarium, Koem.
Family: Zingiberaceae
Eng. Vernac.: Ginger lily

Herbs with perennial, horizontal rhizomatous roots. *Stems* elongated, leafy, 1-1.5 m. *Leaves* canna-like green, pointed, smooth above, pubescent beneath. *Flowers* 7-10 cm across, long tubed, 3 lobed, pure white, very fragrant. *Seed* hard.

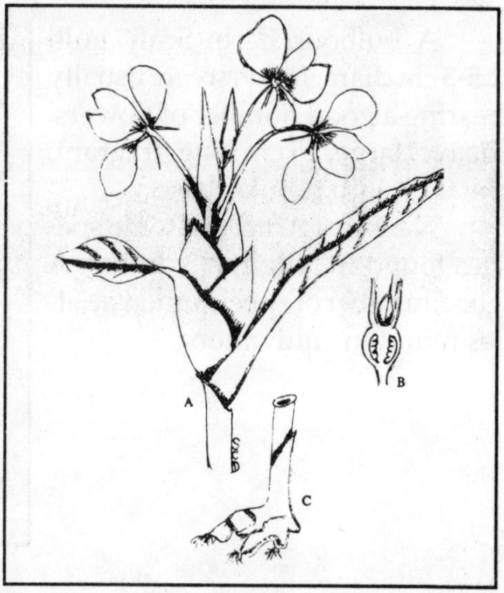

HEDYCHIUM CORONARIUM
A. Shoot with Inflorescence
B. Ovary, Vertical Section C. Roots

Eucharis grandiflora, Planch and Linden

Family: Amaryllidaceae
Eng. vernac: Amazon lily

A bulbous herb, 20-25 cm, leafy through all seasons in moist climate. *Leaves* 30 cm long; flower spike long and hard, terminated with 5-7 flowers. *Flowers* 7 cm across, white, fragrant.

EUCHARIS GRANDIFLORA

Lilium (*L. giganteum*)

Family: Liliaceae
Eng. vernac.: Easter lily

A bulbous herb. Scaly bulb 2.5-3 cm diam. *Inflorescence* usually bearing a good number of flowers. *Flowers* large, 15 cm long, fragrant; petals 6 with tubular base.

Native of America, some species found in Nilgiris (S. India). A good number of species and varieties found in cultivation.

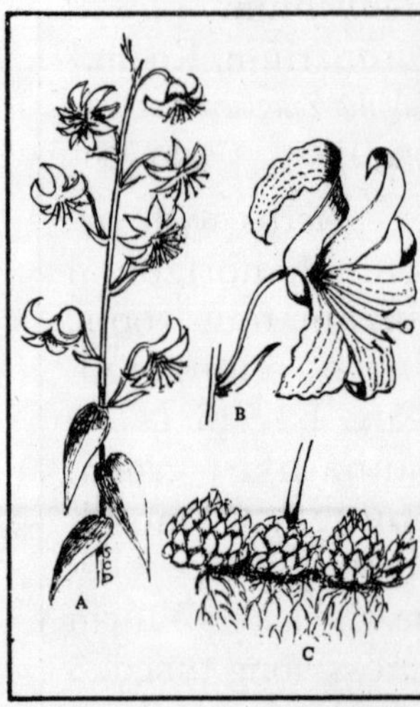

LILIUM
A. Flowering Shoot B. Flower C. Bulbs

ANNUAL HERBS

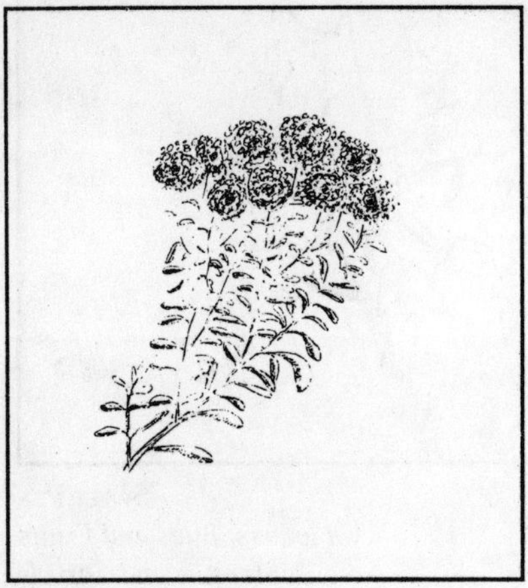

ALYSSUM

Alyssum maritimum, Linn.

Family: Cruciferae
Eng. vernac: Sweet alyssum, Madwort etc.

Very low-growing annual herb with a globular shape. *Leaves* small, simple and light green. *Inflorescence* short with small fragrant flowers, white, rose, deep rose or purple.

Cultivated in gardens.

Dianthus caryophyllus, Linn.

Family: Caryophyllaceae
Eng. vernac: Carnation

Very low-growing annual or biennial herb. Stems characteristically with swollen nodes. *Leaves* opposite, simple, linear. *Flowers* actinomorphic, bi-sexual, petals distinct and free often differentiated into claw. *Stamens* in 1-2 whorls. *Fruit* capsule dehiscing apically by valves; seeds with embryo usually curved.

Cultivated in gardens.

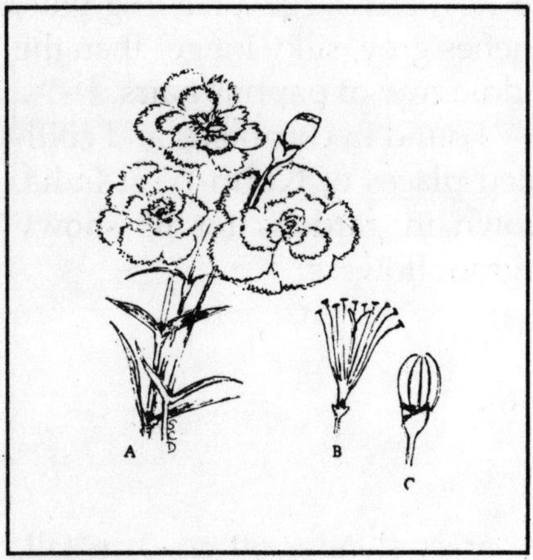

CARNATION
A. Shoots with Flowers
B. Stamens and Carpels C. Fruit

Lathyrus odoratus, Linn.
Eng. vernac.: Sweet pea

A climbing herb. *Stem* rough, hairy, winged. *Leaflets* oval or oblong; stipules lanceolate. *Flowers* in shades of blue, red, yellow and white, fragrant. Pod 25-50 mm, 3-5 seeded.

Cultivated in gardens.

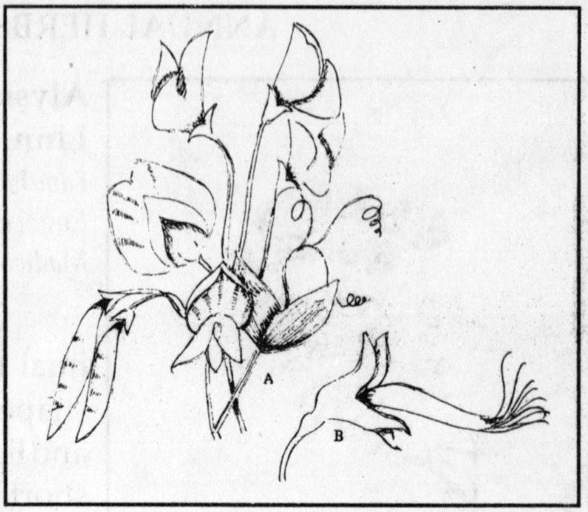

SWEET PEA
A. Flowers, Buds and Fruits
B. Stamens and Carpels

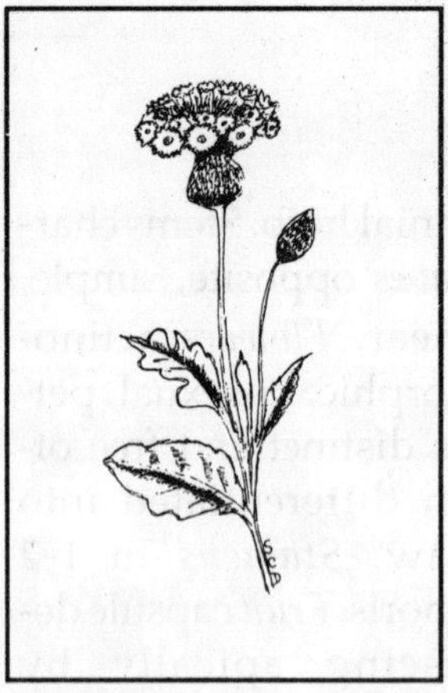

CENTAUREA

Centaurea moschata, Linn.
Family: Compositae
Eng. vernac: Sweet sultan

Annual or biennial, erect, slender. *Leaves* narrow, radial, entire. *Ray florets* large spreading, blue, achenes grey, silky longer than the middle row of pappus hairs.

Found in cornfields and cultivated places of North-West India. Grown in gardens for its showy fragrant flowers.

Nicotiana alata, Linn & Otto.
Family: Solanaceae
Eng. vernac: Flowering tobacco

A biennial herb. *Stem* erect slender 60 cm-3 m tall, branching, *leaves* sessile, oblong-spatulate to ovate, elliptic, apex obtuse, calyx pubescent, corolla villous, night opening, fragrant; tube slender, limb oblique, nearly 50 mm across.

Native of Brazil, Uruguay and Paraguay.

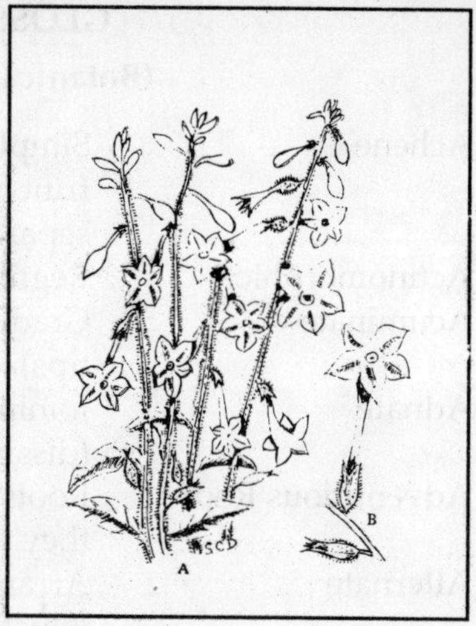

NICOTIANA ALATA
A. Shoots with Buds and Flowers
B. Flower and Fruit

Reseda odorata, Linn.
Family: Resedaceae
Eng. vernac: Mignonette

A biennial herb. *Stem* upright later becoming more or less decumbent and wide-spreading. *Leaves* simple. *Flowers* small, yellow or white in raceme, fragrant.

Cultivated in gardens.

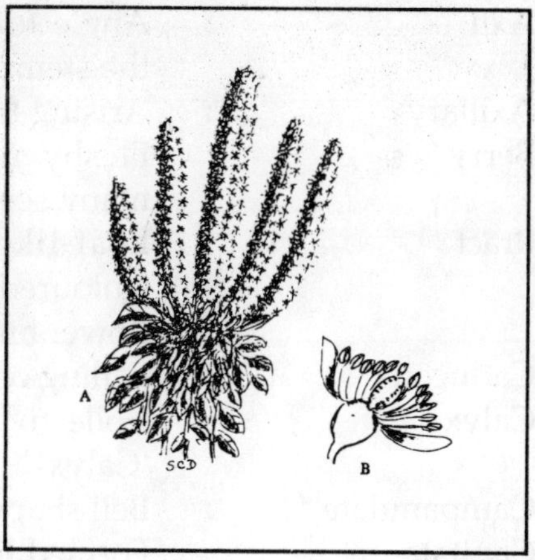

RESEDA
A. Flowering Shoots
B. Flower, Vertical Section

GLOSSARY

(Botanical Terms)

Achene : Simple one-seeded indehiscent dry fruit in which inner seed coat is separate from the outer.

Actinomorphic : Regular, symmetrical.

Acuminate : Gradual narrowing to a point (Leaf tips).

Adnate : Joining of one organ with another (dissimilar).

Adventitious Root : Roots that arise in places where they are not usually found.

Alternate : Arrangement of leaves on stem in which leaves arise simply at each node. Common pattern in plants.

Anthers : Organs bearing pollen sacs.

Anthesis : Period between opening of flowers and setting of fruits.

Axil : Angle formed at the leaf-joint on the stem towards the apex.

Axillary : Arising from axil.

Berry : Fleshy indehiscent fruit having many seeds.

Bract : Leaf-like (green) or petal-like (coloured) organ developed in a flower bunch.

Caducous : Falling off early or prematurely.

Calyx : Collectively sepals are known as 'Calyx'.

Campanulate : Bell shaped.

Capitate : Formed like a head.

Capsule : Dry dehiscent many-seeded fruit.

Carpel : Female reproductive structure bearing and enclosing ovules. Normally comprises an ovary, a style and a stigma.

Connate : Describing similar structures fused with each other, e.g. petals fused to form a tube.

Connivent : Coming together or conversing but not fused.

Cordate : Heart shaped.

Coriaceous : Having a leathery texture.

Corolla : Collectively petals are known as 'Corolla'.

Corymb : A flower-bunch in which stalks of flowers are of different lengths, the lowermost flower has longest stalk and the uppermost has shortest one.

Cyme : In a flower-bunch apex of main axis terminates with a flower; then new flowers arise from laterals repeatedly.

Deciduous : Falling at the end of growing season.

Decumbent : Reclining or lying on the ground, but with the end ascending.

Dentate : Describing leaf-margins that are toothed with outward pointing notches.

Didymous : Describing arrangement of anthers which are in two pairs.

Distichous : Two-ranked leaflets or flowers on opposite sides of a stem.

Dorsifixed : Describing an anther joined to the filament for some distance along its dorsal edge.

Enciform : Sword shaped.

Fascicle : A condensed or close cluster.

Filament : Stalk of a stamen bearing anther at the apex.

Follicle : Dry dehiscent fruit developing from

		unilocular ovary having many seeds.
Glabrascent	:	Partly glossy and partly hairy.
Glabrous	:	A surface that is smooth, devoid of hairs.
Glandular	:	Having glands of one or many cells which secrete special chemical substances.
Imbricated	:	Overlapping, as shingles on a roof.
Imparipinnate	:	A feather-like leaf having single terminal leaflet at the apical end of main axis.
erior Ovary	:	Ovary of a flower, which remains below the level of sepals, petals and stamens.
Inflorescence	:	Flower bunch in which flowers are arranged on an axis.
Introrse	:	Anthers that burst towards the centre of the flower thus promoting self-pollination.
Lanceolate	:	Narrow and tapering at both of its ends.
Monocot	:	Having one seed-leaf.
Oblanceolate	:	The reverse of lanceolate; broader towards the apex, not at the middle as in the lanceolate.
Obtuse	:	Leaf apex that is blunt or rounded in shape.
Ovary	:	An organ that contains ovule/ovules that becomes/become seed embryo after fertilization.
Palmate	:	Palm shaped leaf in which leaflets arise from a single point.
Panicle	:	Flower bunch having flowers with stalks.
Paniculate	:	Resembling a panicle.
Pappus	:	Modified petals that are made up ot a ring of fine hairs, scales or teeth.

Pectinate	:	Comb-like with very close narrow divisions.
Pedicel	:	The stalk that attaches a flower to the main axis of the flower bunch.
Peltate	:	A circular leaf with its stalk in its centre.
Pendulous	:	Hanging like a pendulum.
Perennial	:	A plant that lives for many years.
Perianth	:	Any substitute of petals that protects the reproductive organs.
Plano-concave	:	One side is plane and the opposite side is concave.
Pubescent	:	Having fine short hairs.
Raceme	:	A type of flower bunch in which flowers are formed on individual pedicel on the main.
Ray Floret	:	Florets having broad petals usually arranged at the other row of a flower head as in sunflower.
Reniform	:	Kidney shaped.
Rhomboid	:	The shape of a rhombus (quadrilateral).
Salver shaped	:	From a narrow point an abruptly expanded flat limb as in the petals of *vinca*.
Sepal	:	Green structure that covers and protects the floral parts in the bud stage.
Serrate	:	A leaf margin that is toothed with forward pointing notches.
Sessile	:	Having no stalk.
Spadix	:	A flower bunch in which flowers are sessile and borne on a fleshy and enlarged axis, usually surrounded by a large bract or sheath.
Spathe	:	A large sheath that encloses a spadix, may be highly coloured and petaloid.

Stamen	:	Male reproductive organ.
Stigma	:	The tip of a carpel that receives pollens.
Stilt Root	:	A form of prop root. An adventitious root that provides additional support to the plant.
Stipule	:	Leaf-like structure, usually in pairs; may be spines, glands or scales at the leaf base or along the petiole.
Ternate	:	In 3's.
Tomentose	:	Surface densely covered with short hairs.
Trichotomous	:	3-pronged-like divisions.
Trifoliate	:	A compound leaf having three leaflets.
Tumid	:	Swollen, inflated.
Valvate	:	Petals or sepals in which individual units are arranged in circle, their edges just touching each other but not overlapping in the bud.
Villous	:	Provided with long and soft, not matted, hairs; shaggy.

2

Horticulture

This part of the book deals with the agro-technique for growing fragrant flowers in home gardens and commercial fields. All the cultivars have their growing technique for home gardens. For commercial culture only those cultivars have been dealt with, which have commercial importance either as cut-flower or for perfume extraction. There are however certain species which are exploited for both the purposes of cut-flower and perfume extraction.

The agro-technique comprises soil and culture, i.e., ground preparation, propagation, cultural operations, application of feed supplements etc. Protection against pests and diseases has also been dealt with laying due emphasis.

SOIL AND CULTURE

Soil

The soil suitable for agricultural purposes has three basic ingredients—clay particles, silt particles and sand grains. Obviously these materials are in varying proportions in different soil samples. The type of soil texture is to indicate the ratio of the basic ingredients in a particular soil sample.

Texture: The soil samples are classified into two main groups, light and heavy. The clay particles are very fine. On the contrary the sand grains are coarse. Hence a soil containing more clay is termed as 'fine textured' soil. 'Coarse textured' soils are those which contain more sand. Silt is a quartzic substance lying between sand and clay. A loam which is neither light nor heavy contains equal amounts of clay and sand. To indicate the different texture the terms used are 'heavy soil', 'light soil', 'loam', 'light loam', etc.

A heavy soil or clay is sticky, not porous and does not permit the percolation of water through the soil mass. On the contrary light or sandy soil is very porous, which facilitates the percolation of water rapidly. Hence it does not pose any problem of drainage. A light soil runs dry quickly and needs more irrigation. A heavy soil is just the opposite.

Structure: A soil or compost of an improved structure is highly suitable for the root growth. The friable and granular structure of a soil is considered to be an improved condition which is achieved by adding sufficient quantities of humus to it. For adding humus to the compost leafmould, farmyard manure or cow-manure is used. Soil structure can also be improved by adding lime. Even a clay soil can be made granular by liming. The granulation of a soil facilitates aeration and drainage.

Acidity

Liming can reduce the acidity of a soil and increase its alkalinity. Generally 50 grams of chalk (pulverised) should be applied per square metre of garden space.

Plant Food

Plants take some elements as food for their growth and development from the soil. Those elements are nitrogen, phosphorus, potassium, sulphur, calcium and magnesium, as well as iron, manganese, sodium, chlorine and silicon. There are few more elements which are required in traces. They are copper, molybdenum, zinc, boron etc.

These elements however cannot be utilised in their original form. They form selective compounds which are absorbed by the plants.

Plants take nitrogen as nitrate or ammonia. Similarly plants use phosphorus as phosphates and potassium, calcium and magnesium as their salts. All these chemical compounds which are absorbed and utilised by the plants for their growth are regarded as plant food.

Manures

Many substances, both organic and inorganic, are used as manures and fertilizers to feed plants.

All organic matter, dead or excreted, when decomposed can supply plant nutrients. Hence organic matter must undergo decomposition before it can be used as a manure. Leaves, barks, twigs, fruit peels, seeds, straws and grasses become manure on decomposition. But hoof and horn, leather, bone, if pulverised, can be applied to the soil. Similarly dry fish can be a good manure. Oil seeds, after oil extraction, form a cake which is regarded as a manure.

Fertilizers

Many chemical substances contain plant nutrients. Certain compounds are however commercially manufactured in bulk for use as fertilizers. Such products are urea, super phosphate, muriate of potash, calcium ammonium nitrate (CAN), potassium sulphate, etc. In this country the use of chemical fertilizers has increased. Many gardeners are still not in favour of using chemical substances for feeding their plants. But a remarkable result is obtained in growth and production when fertilizers are used with plenty of organic manures. The following chemical compounds are used as fertilizers.

Urea: It is a concentrated nitrogenous fertilizer which contains 45 per cent of nitrogen. Urea contains only nitrogen and nothing else. It can be used during soil preparation and as top dressing or liquid manure for the growing plants.

Ammonium sulphate: Plants obtain 21 per cent of nitrogen from this fertilizer. It also supplies sulphur. Before the introduction of urea this fertilizer was the main source of nitrogen for plants in a chemical form. Now its use is very limited. But it is highly recommended for alkaline soils, because alkalinity is reduced by its acid reaction. Obviously, it should not be used in acidic soil.

Calcium ammonium nitrate: Also known as 'CAN', it contains 20 per cent of nitrogen and can be used as top dressing or in the preparation of soil.

Ammonium nitrate: It contains 35 per cent of nitrogen. But half of this amount is available in the nitrate form and the other half in the ammonium form. No other fertilizer except urea contains so much nitrogen.

Di-ammonium phosphate: It contains 18 per cent of nitrogen and 48 per cent of phosphate. Its abbreviated name is D.A.P.

Super phosphate: It contains phosphorus penta oxide (P_2O_5) from which plants get phosphorus. It is of two kinds—single and triple. The first contains 16-18 per cent of phosphate and 19 per cent of calcium.

Rock phosphate: This type of phosphate has been found in a number of rocks in India. Two rock phosphates — 'Musouri Phos' and 'Purulia Phos' are marketed as fertilizers. Rock phosphate is very useful for acidic soils, because it contains more calcium. Its phosphate becomes soluble in acids. Therefore, it should not be used in alkaline soils. Plants can absorb the total amount of phosphate from rock phosphates. Besides, some trace elements are also available.

Muriate of potash: It contains 80-85 per cent of potassium chloride and 15-20 per cent of common salt. Its potash content is very high, yet it should not be used for growing roses. Because its common salt is reacted to form sodium carbonate in the soil, which is harmful to roses.

Sulphate of potash: It contains 50-54 per cent of pure potash (K_2O). It becomes easily soluble in water and is readily absorbed by plants, and not easily leached out from the soil. The sulphate of potash produced in India is used as a laboratory chemical. For its use as a fertilizer it is imported from other countries. For growing quality tobacco sulphate of potash is essential. Hence, the whole of the imported material is distributed in the tobacco growing areas.

Sources of Other Nutrients

	Percentage (%)
Calcium:	
Limestone	40
Quicklime	71
Slaked lime	54
Plaster of Paris	23
Super phosphate	19
Dolomite (a form of lime)	30
Magnesium:	
Dolomite	21
Magnesium sulphate	20
(also known as Mag sulf or Epsom Salt)	
Sulphur:	
Ammonium sulphate	24
Gypsum (Plaster of Paris)	18
Super phosphate	8-13
Boron:	
Borax	11
Boric acid	14
Iron:	
Iron sulphate	20
Manganese:	
Manganese sulphate	36
Manganous oxide	77
Molybdenum:	
Sodium molybdate	36
Zinc:	
Zinc sulphate	36
Zinc oxide	79

Soil Preparation

Before planting the garden soil should be prepared so

that the plants can have nourishment for their proper growth and development. It should be borne in mind that different types of plants need different types of soil depth for spreading their roots.

For the required tilth the soil should be spaded out accordingly. After having the required tilth, manure and fertilizer should be mixed to the soil. Generally cow-manure or farmyard manure is used to improve the soil structure. Use one cubic metre of manure per 20 square metres of bed. To supplement phosphate and potash, super phosphate of lime and sulphate of potash are used respectively. If sulphate of potash is not available muriate of potash can be used as a substitute.

Spread the manure uniformly over the bed. Then sprinkle a mixture of 200 grams of single super phosphate of lime and 100 grams of sulphate of potash per square metre over it. Now mix the manure and fertilizers thoroughly with soil of the tilth by spading. Leave the soil in a moist condition for a week before planting.

It should be borne in mind that the bed thus prepared does not contain sufficient nitrogen as supplements. Hence to make it rich in nitrogen the required amount of oil cake or hoof and hornmeal or both should be mixed with the soil; 250 grams of oil cake (mustard, *neem* or groundnut) or 100 grams of hoof and hornmeal should be the quantity of manure per square metre. Oil cake takes around three weeks to be decomposed. Hence in the process of mixing cow-manure, oil cake or/and hoof and hornmeal should be mixed first with the soil. After two weeks the fertilizers as recommended are applied. For its decomposition oil cake needs moisture in the soil.

Making Pits (for trees, shrubs or climbers)

As the saplings of trees, shrubs or climbers are planted at a distance from each other pits, instead of beds, are required for them. Pits are dug out at the points marked for planting. In each pit one sapling is planted. The dimensions of a pit should be of 45 cm diameter and 45-60 cm depth. Three-fourths of the soil heaped near the pit should be mixed with one basketful of cow-manure, 100 grams of super phosphate and 50 grams of muriate of potash. Then fill in the pit with this manured soil. To make it more fertile add 200 grams of pulverised oilcake (mustard or *neem*) to the soil and mix it thoroughly. Leave the pit in a moist condition for three weeks before planting.

Potting Compost

For growing plants in pots a good potting compost is required. A few mixtures are given below, which can be used with advantage.

(For 8 plants in 30 cm pots)

1

Heavy loam	45 litres
Cow-manure	15 litres
Leafmould	5 litres
Urea	100 grams
Bonemeal	200 grams
Sulphate of potash	30 grams

2

Clay	35 litres
Sand	15 litres
Cow-manure/compost	15 litres
Ammonium sulphate	250 grams

3

Loam	45 litres
Leafmould	20 litres
Hoof and hornmeal	1 kg
Di-ammonium phosphate (D.A.P.)	300 grams
Muriate of potash	100 grams
Magnesium sulphate	5 grams

4

Clay (Heavy soil)	25 litres

Sand	15 litres
Cow-manure/compost	15 litres
Rallimeal/Sterameal	500 grams

5

Loam	49 litres
Cow-manure/compost	20 litres
Rallimeal/Sterameal	500 grams

6

Clay (Heavy soil)	45 litres
Cow-manure/compost	20 litres
Oil cake (mustard, *neem* or groundnut)	1 kg
Super phosphate	100 grams
Magnesium sulphate	50 grams

(Note: The clay, cow-manure and pulverised oil cake should be mixed thoroughly and stacked in a moist condition for a month; then all the ingredients should be mixed together.)

7

Loam	45 litres
Oil cake (mustard, *neem* or groundnut)	1 kg
Di-ammonium phosphate (D.A.P.)	300 grams
Muriate of potash	100 grams
Magnesium sulphate	50 grams

(Note: The mixing is same as that of the compost No. 6.)

Planting

The planting of seedlings in ground is a very common practice. The pot plants may also be transferred to the ground. Seedlings or cuttings grown in small pots are also transplanted in ground for flowering. The seedlings, cuttings or grafts of shrubs or trees are also grown in pots in their early stage of growth. Later, they find their permanent position in the ground. In planting out the following tips are helpful:

i) The bed or pits of suitable tilth should be prepared beforehand (see soil preparation).
ii) In a dry soil planting should not be done. The soil should be in a moist condition at the time of planting. Too wet a soil must not be touched.
iii) The distance from plant to plant and row to row should be determined and markings for the position of the plants should be made on the bed accordingly.
iv) For an individual plant make a hole of required dimensions on the planting position marked beforehand.
v) Prick out the seedlings or take out the plants with the root ball from the pots carefully.
vi) Plant as usual. Too deep or shallow planting is not advisable. The plant should stand erect, not inclined.
vii) Plants having weak stems need staking (see 'Staking & Tying').
viii) Water the plants with the water can fitted with a fine rose.
ix) While pricking out, the seedlings part with some of their roots. Hence they will take time to be established. To cure them rapidly protection from the strong sun must be provided. A paper bag or flowerpot inverted over each plant can protect it from the sun.

Potting

House plants are mostly grown in pots. Those who have no garden space can grow ornamental shrubs and herbs in pots. They can enjoy both garden and gardening in their verandahs or on their rooftops. Considering the advantage of moving a pot plant to a desired spot growers are inclined to pot culture.

A flowerpot must have drain hole at its bottom. Before filling the pot with compost it must be crocked, i.e., a piece of broken pot should be placed over the drain hole with its concave side facing downward. Place a layer (3.5 cm thick) of grit or stone chips over the crock. Then sprinkle dry sand over the layer of grit. The sand will fill up the void in between the grits. This layer of aggregate (grit and sand) will separate the pot soil from the drain hole thus facilitating the drainage of surplus water from the pot soil.

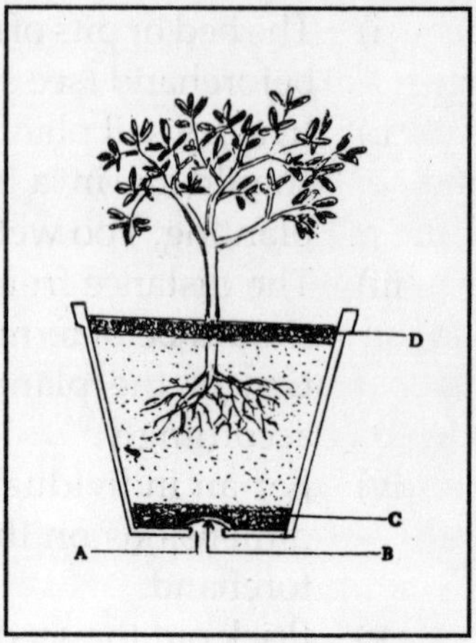

POTTING
A. Drain Hole B. Crock
C. Layer of Grit and Sand
D. Mulch

At the time of potting the compost should be in a moist condition. Fill in one-third of the empty space of the pot with the compost (see 'Potting Compost'). If the plant is too small the compost level should be raised by adding more compost. The plant might be with bare roots or soil ball. In the case of the bare-root plant hold the plant with the left hand and spread the roots over the compost. Then cover the roots with compost with the right hand. Press the soil round the plant so that there is no void in the soil mass. Leave 3 cm space empty at the top for holding water. After potting water copiously with a water can until some amount of water is drained out through the drain hole. Place the potted plant in a shade until its roots take soil, which will be indicated by the resumption of foliage growth. The re-potting of a pot plant with a root ball is rather easy. Place the root ball on the cushion of the compost at a desired height. Then fill in the sides with the compost, other operations remaining same as for bare-root plants.

Watering

Plants cannot do without water. Hence water the plants as needed. 'No more, no less' is the golden rule. But this can be learnt by experience. The amount of water needed depends on the amount of foliage, humidity of the air, air current, day temperature and soil texture. In a moist atmosphere the rate of evaporation of water from the soil surface and through the leaf pores decreases. In such a condition the plants need less water. On the contrary, hot dry winds increase the need of water by plants for the excessive loss of water through the leaf pores (stoma). The coarse textured soil runs dry quickly. It cannot retain moisture for a long time. Due to its porous nature water percolates, going beyond the root zone. On the other hand, a heavy soil can hold moisture for a long time. A clay soil is heavy and fine textured.

Watering with the Fine Rose of a Water Can

i) Pot plants need almost daily watering. Water them when necessary. Use a water can with a fine spout.
ii) Ground plants need irrigation at an interval of 3-15 days.
iii) Flood irrigation with a hose pipe once a week as a common practice for ground plants.
iv) The surface of the bed exposed to sun and air is crusted which prevents percolation of water. Hence a few hours before watering the crusted soil should be forked in. If the soil is mulched (see 'Mulching') no forking is necessary.
v) Irrigate the soil when needed. This is learnt by experience. Over-watering and dry condition are both harmful to plants.
vi) The best watering time is around the evening. But pot plants should be watered when necessary.

Staking and Tying

Most of the ornamental herbs have weak stems. So they need support to stand erect. Shrubs including roses are hardly staked. But the standard or tree rose invariably needs a strong staking. For this purpose iron conduit (pipe) is most suitable. The wooden, bamboo or reed stakes that remain with the plants for more than a season may be destroyed by white ants, for which the plant may suffer breakage. To keep them at bay the stakes may be treated with aldrin, creosite oil or painted with tar. Aesthetically, staking should be unobtrusive. For tying the stems to the canes a very pliable twine is used. The tying must be a bit loose, for a tight tying may cut into the stems. Although iron stakes (tubes, rods or angles) can be used for tying no wire should be used.

Mulching

Mulching consists of a layer of coarse manure applied on the soil surface around the base of the plants. It serves many purposes, and is considered an important operation of cultivation. A mulch prevents the baking of the top soil exposed to sun and air. No forking is required after mulching. Feeding through liquid manure or top dressing is also facilitated by mulching. The spread of a mulch should correspond to that of the plant. The suitable materials for mulching are cow-manure, compost, leafmould etc. The chopped or decomposed straw can also be used for the purpose.

Feeding

The manures and fertilizers used in preparing soil or potting compost cannot sustain the plant growth for a long time with important food elements. However rich a soil may be certain elements are likely to run short before long. Amongst them nitrogen is most fleeing, especially in sandy soil. It is easily leached out and goes beyond the root zone of the plants. Hence nitrogen has to be replenished at short intervals during the growing season. The supplemental feed is applied in three ways, i.e., top dressing, liquid manure and foliar feeding. Although basically same they are applied in different ways.

Top dressing: Generally, chemical fertilizers or a mixture of chemical and organic materials of nutritive value are used as a top dressing. It is useful to ground plants as well as pot plants. A top dressing is applied after forking the soil round the plants and it must be followed by a good irrigation. Top dressings are applied at an interval of 4-8 weeks during the season. The following mixtures are suitable as top dressing for different flower crops:

1

Cow-manure/compost	5 buckets (5 litre capacity)
Neem cake (pulverised)	1 kg
Bonemeal	250 grams
Wood ash	250 grams

2

Cow-manure/compost	50 litres
Mustard cake (pulverised)	500 grams
Bonemeal	250 grams
Hoof and hornmeal	250 grams
Sulphate of potash	100 grams

3

Cow-manure/compost	50 litres
Mustard cake (pulverised)	500 grams
Urea	70 grams
Super phosphate (single)	300 grams
Muriate of potash	100 grams

4

Cow-manure/compost	50 litres
Sterameal/Rallimeal	1.5 kgs

Any of the above mixtures can be applied in a space of 2-4 square metres of a flower bed. Normally, a top dressing does not contain magnesium, calcium, iron, etc. In case the deficiency of such nutrients is evident, attempts are made to replenish them by foliar feed or liquid manure.

Liquid manure: Plants can absorb nutrients rapidly from a liquid manure. When deficiency symptoms are apparent manure in a liquid form should be applied. The materials for preparing a liquid manure should be chosen with a view to making it a balanced fertilizer. Nitrogen being the main element of a liquid manure the ingredients used should be both organic and chemical. A few of the mixtures which can be used as liquid manure are given below:

1

Mustard cake	200 grams
CAN (calcium ammonium nitrate)	50 grams
Magnesium sulphate	10 grams
Water	10 litres

2

Mustard cake	200 grams
Urea	25 grams
Sulphate of potash	20 grams
Magnesium sulphate	10 grams
Water	10 litres

3

Mustard cake/groundnut cake	200 grams
Di-ammonium phosphate (D.A.P.)	100 grams
Sulphate of potash	20 grams
Magnesium sulphate	10 grams
Water	10 litres

4

Di-ammonium phosphate (D.A.P.)	100 grams
Sulphate of potash	20 grams
Magnesium sulphate	10 grams
Water	10 litres

Preparation: Soak the oilcake in 5 litres of water for a week or so. Then soak calcium ammonium nitrate or di-ammonium phosphate for 8-10 hours in a litre of water. Mix these liquids and other ingredients together. Add more water (4 litres) to make it a manure of 10 litres.

This 10 litre manure can be applied to a flower bed of 1-2 square metre area. Care should be taken to see that liquid manure is not applied on a dry surface. It is safe to water the plants before applying the manure.

Foliar Feeding

A plant can be fed through leaves. Certain nutrients due to complex soil reactions cannot be used by plants. To get rid of this trouble nutrient mixtures in a liquid form are straightway applied on the leaves by spraying. Generally the trace elements or micro-nutrients are fed through leaves. The foliar feeds are of two types — some for the main elements and others for the trace elements. They are also used separately and should not be mixed together.

Nowadays proprietary products which can be used as foliar feed are available in the market. They should be used as per the directions of their manufacturers. A list of popular products is given below:

Product	*Producers*
Agromin	Arries Agrovet Industrial Products Ltd., Bombay-43
Tracel-2	Rallis India Ltd., Bangalore-54
Multiplex	Karnatak Agro Chemicals, Bangalore-10
Micronutrient Mix	Pausak Ltd., Baroda-3
Vipul	Godrej Boecy
Trasco-5	Super Agro India, 22B, Satchasi Para Rd., Calcutta-700 002

Hoeing and Weeding

On going through 'mulching' and 'watering' a question may crop up why and when hoeing is necessary. Hoeing helps break the crusted layer caused mainly by sun-baking. If not forked the surface soil gradually becomes impervious to water and air. The roots need both

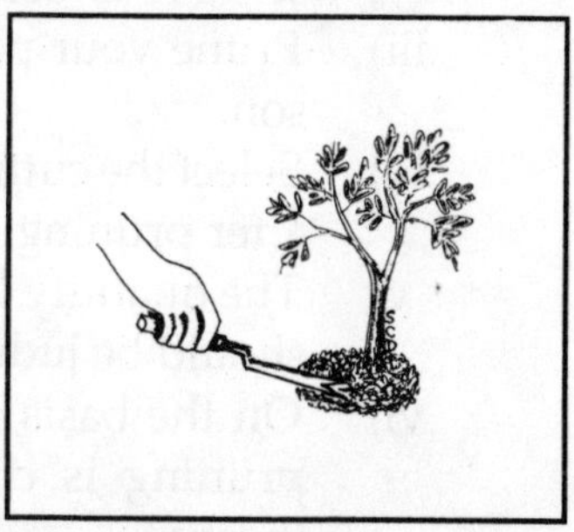

FORKING

water and air to maintain their growth. The soil microbes that cause many useful changes in the soil also need aeration. So forking the top soil round the base of the plants is essential.

Fork the soil before watering. It should be done once a week. Deep forking is not recommended. For the bulbous crop the forking should be carefully done so that it does not cause any injury to the bulbs or tubers formed underground.

Hoeing and weeding should go hand in hand. The beds or pots must be kept weed-free.

Pruning

The pruning of branches of flower plants is essential for those cultivars which flower better on the new growths of the season. Secondly, pruning also helps keep the plants within bounds. Thirdly, to maintain a balance between the vegetative and floral growths pruning is imperative.

Some cultivars which need annual pruning are listed below. The time of pruning in the plains is also mentioned.

Cultivars	*Pruning time*
Rose	October-November
Quisqualis	January-February
Sambac	January-February
Cestrum	December-January

i) Pruning obviously refers to the removal of plant parts as a part of the cultural operations.
ii) It is done with a very sharp knife, a pair of scissors or secateurs.
iii) Prune your plants just before the growing season.
iv) Select the cutting point just above the bud so that after pruning the bud can start growing.
v) The quantity of wood to be removed by pruning should be judiciously considered.
vi) On the basis of the amount of wood removed, pruning is classified as 'light', 'medium', or 'heavy'.

vii) Heavy pruning makes the plant weaker and it takes a long time to cover with branches and foliage. On the other hand, the light pruning helps put forth a number of shoots to cover the plant quickly. The effect of medium pruning lies between heavy and light pruning.

viii) The cut end is susceptible to fungous attacks. So care should be taken to apply Chaubattia paint over the cut surface. Bavistin paste (Bavistin + water) is also very effective. Besides red lead, wood ash or fresh cowdung is also used. Bordeaux paste is also recommended for the purpose (see also PRUNING a rose in this chapter).

PLANT PROPAGATION

Flower plants are multiplied from seeds, shoots or roots, i.e., new plants can be raised through seeds or vegetative parts. Vegetative parts like leaves, shoots, roots etc. are employed in propagating plants. The plants dealt with here are multiplied vegetatively by cuttings, layers, grafts or bulbs.

Cutting

Jasmine, gardenia, plumeria etc. are propagated by shoot cuttings. Those which are herbaceous are propagated by soft cuttings. On the contrary the woody plants are grown from hard wood cuttings. There are however certain trees and shrubs which can be

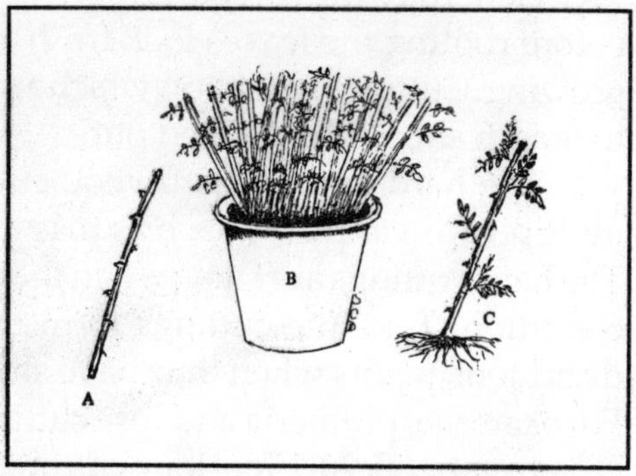

ROSE CUTTINGS (HARD)
A. Cutting B. Inserted in the Pot C. After Rooting

propagated by soft-wood cuttings, e.g., Pterospermum, Gardenia etc.

Soft twigs, 4-8 cm long, are cut with a sharp shaving blade. The cut should preferably be made just below a leaf joint. A hormone powder such as Seradix B_1 (or any good substitute) should be applied at the cut end to stimulate rooting.

Fine aggregates free from soil particles are suitable as a rooting medium. Generally clean, coarse sand collected fresh from its source is considered superior to other materials. A shallow seed pan of 30 cm diameter with a few drain holes at the bottom is suitably used as a container of the medium. Before filling the pan with sand crock the holes so that the sand cannot pass through them. Water copiously to soak the sand thoroughly. To insert the base of the cuttings make holes in the sand with a pointed wood pencil and the like. The holes should not be deeper than 15 mm. Put one cutting in each hole and press the sand about it. Water gently to settle the sand around the cuttings. Place the pots in a shady and airy corner of the garden. The morning sun is very helpful. So a regular exposure to it up to 8 a.m. is recommended. The occasional exposure to rains is not harmful, rather refreshing and stimulating, hence useful.

Generally the soft cuttings take 1-3 weeks to root. Just before rooting the leaves look fresh and the tips seem to be growing. Cuttings with roots which are only a few centimetres in length should be pricked out.

The hard or semi-hardwood cuttings are employed to multiply flower plants such as rose, gardenia, plumeria etc. The hard cuttings are taken when the plants are in a dormant condition. Take the cuttings from the deciduous or semi-deciduous plants when they have shed most of their leaves. For example, plumeria and rose cuttings are taken in winter.

In general, 20-25 cm long cuttings of pencil thickness are taken from the branches with sharp knife or secateurs. While preparing them, the base of the cuttings must be marked, otherwise there is a danger of the top of the cuttings being inserted wrongly into the rooting medium. For the hardwood or semi-hardwood cuttings Seradix B_3 and B_2 (or any good substitute) are used respectively. The application of rooting hormone not only hastens root eruption but also increases the chances of success and the number of roots. As a rooting medium loam or pure sand can be used. The cuttings should be inserted 3-4 cm deep in the medium. If the cuttings are taken in winter they need not be put under the shade. The cuttings from deciduous plants in winter strike well in full sun. The hardwood cuttings can also be inserted in the ground.

Layering

This is also a method of vegetative propagation. The layerings are of two types—ground layering and air layering. The layering is an extensive method of propagation of flowering shrubs. The ground layering is practised in case of climbers and those plants which have long flexible or trailing stems. Carnation, though herbaceous, is propagated by ground layering. When cuttings do not root satisfactorily layering is the answer. The rate of success in layering is more because the layered shoot, unlike the cuttings, enjoys the supply of water and nourishment from the mother plant until it can depend on its own roots.

Air layering: A shoot about 30 cm long is selected for layering. A griddle is made at a point 20-30 cm from the tip to remove a ring of bark, 15-20 mm wide. Then scrape the silvery portion of the exposed wood to prevent healing. To hasten rooting apply suitable root-hormone powder on the top cut of the bark. About 100 grams of moist sphagnum is placed around the stem to enclose the cut surface. Hold the moss ball in position and get it wrapped up with a piece of alkathene film (20 x 25 cm). The two ends must be twisted and tied with a piece of *sutli* (hessian cord) so that no water can seep inside. If layering is tried in the humid period of the year 2-6 week time is generally needed for rooting. The growing roots can be seen through the alkathene film. After detaching the layer from the mother plant remove the alkathene film and transplant it in a pot. Then place the pot in a shady corner until the roots take soil.

Ground layering: This is done by bending the flexible long cane of shrubs or climbers to the ground and covering it partially with soil leaving the top portion exposed and in vertical position. In many cultivars which do not grow roots easily a notch or a tongue is made at the under side of the stem lying in the ground. To fix the layered portion to the ground a peg or a block of stone is used. The tongue or the notch may be treated with a hormone powder for early rooting. The soil must be kept moist until the rooted layer is removed and potted. The new layer should be treated as the rooted cuttings of the same type of cultivars.

Division of clump: Cultivars like jasmine, cestrum, clematis etc. can be multiplied by division of a clump. In such plants a clump is formed by a good number of offshoots. Each of them usually has its own roots. By removing the soil from the sides of the clump offshoots are separated from the mother plant. Then they are treated as rooted cuttings, and those without roots are as good as blanched cuttings which in general root earlier than usual.

Storage Roots

Storage roots and stems are in common parlance called bulbs. Bulbs, tubers, corms and rhizomes tend to remain in a dormant condition during winter.

Bulbs: Tuberose, lilium, eucaris etc. are propagated by bulbs. The bulbs form bulblets. From growing or dormant plants bulblets can be separated and planted for getting new plants.

Rhizome: Hedychium, orchid etc. are propagated by their rhizomatous roots. The rhizome can be divided into a number of sections, each having at least one shoot or sprout.

Grafting

In grafting two different plant species are required for making a desired type. In general, a delicate species does not form any strong root system from its vegetative parts. Hence grafting is the only answer; because in grafting the shoots (scion) of a mother plant are grafted onto stocks bearing stronger roots, which must be a closely related species. For example, for grafting the rose of a garden variety a wild rose is required as rootstock.

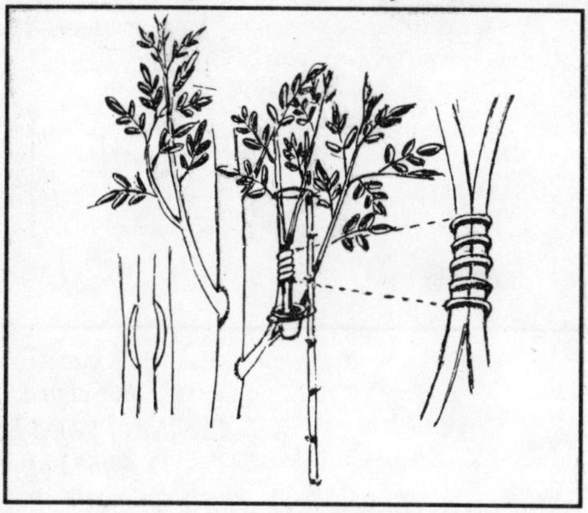

INARCHING (APPROACH GRAFTING)

Approach Grafting: It is the oldest process of grafting and is also known as 'inarching'. Before the introduction of bud grafting inarching was the only process of grafting. In approach grafting both the stock and the scion grow independently on their own roots. To bring about union at the point of contact a slice of wood (4-5 cm long) half of the thickness from each of the stock and the scion is removed carefully with a sharp knife. The union should be tied tightly with a suitable cord. After healing of the cut surface the graft is separated from the mother plant. In this operation the top of the stock and the base of the scion are gradually severed. On separation the new graft should be provided with a stake and be kept in a partially shady place for a week or so after potting.

Budding

It is a kind of grafting which is done conveniently keeping the mother plant and the stock at a distance from each other. A rootstock of a closely related species is selected, i.e., the stock and the scion plant must belong to the same family. That is not all, even the individuals of the same family should be closely related.

Propagation of the modern rose is mainly done by

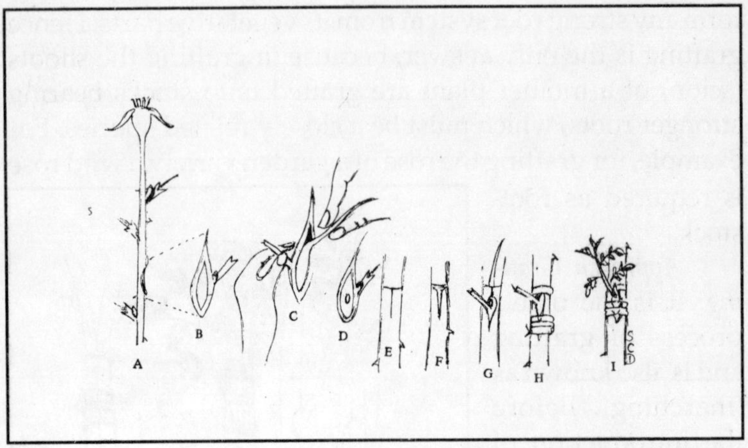

SHIELD BUDDING

A. Scion with Trimmed Leaves B. Shield
C. Slice of Wood being detached from the Shield
D. Shield after detaching the Slice of Wood
E. Rootstock with a 'T'-Cut F. Bark Loosened to hold the Shield
G. Shield put in position H. Shield tied in I. Growing Bud

budding. Generally, rootstocks are grown by cuttings. The common type of budding is known as 'T' budding or shield budding. A cross-cut is first made on the stem, just deep enough to cut the bark 2-4 cm above the ground level. Then starting about 2 cm below make a vertical cut to meet the first cut to form a 'T'. To loosen the bark give the knife a slight twist on either side for making room for the bud. Collect a scion with 'eyes' from the shoot that has a bloom which has just faded or withered. The term 'eye' is to mean the bud of a leaf joint. Trim the leaf stalks about one centimetre above the joints. Then remove the thorns, if any, by snapping them off. With the sharp blade of a budding knife lift the bud with a slice of wood of the scion. The wood portion under the 'eye' should be removed carefully without bruising the shield. The trimmed leaf stalk which is one centimetre long will serve as a handle of the shield. Holding the handle insert the shield into the T-shaped cut and tie it carefully with an alkathene strip starting from below and working upwards leaving the 'eye' itself uncovered.

Within 2-3 weeks the bud will swell as a sign of growth after the bud union has taken place. Remove all the shoots below the bud and trim the head of the stock to force the bud to grow. In the first instalment remove only the twigs. In the second and final stage when the bud grows to a shoot of 3-4 cm long, cut back the stock 2-3 cm above the bud joint.

GARDENS FOR THE BLIND

The blinds are gifted with a strong smelling organ that helps them to perceive even a feeble smell. So in their case the nose serves as a substitute for eyes. There are fragrant gardens in a number of developed countries which are mainly for the blind. The first of this type was set up in 1939 in Exeter (England). The next in Lima pa (USA) in 1949. Besides there are two such gardens which are given below:

1955	Brukleen Botanical Garden	New York City
1956	Light House	Chicago City

These gardens have their arrangements for the blind to recognize the plants. Each plant has its name label written in the braille system near the base so that a blind can read it by the finger touch over the braille. The garden paths are laid out in a way which are convenient for the blind to move about.

INDOOR GARDENING WITH FRAGRANT FLOWERS

Indoor gardening with fragrant flowers has a special charm. Although people resort to raising house plants in the absence of open space for gardening for the scented flowers, however, proximity for inhaling perfume is an utmost necessity. Hence despite enough garden spaces growing herds of house plants bearing flowers has its significance.

It is said that indoor gardening is never out of season. The recent trend of having house plants which can thrive at homes finds its another utility in indoor decorations. So indoor gardening with fragrant flowers satisfies three-fold needs—close association with plants and flowers, enjoyment of sweet perfume and indoor decorations.

The ancient Greeks and Romans were fond of growing plants indoors. The Scandinavians and Americans are the pioneers in indoor gardening. The modern architectural designing of houses and flats makes the rooms well lighted with larger windows fitted with glass panes. Similarly the staircase with vertically long glass panels facilitates incoming of direct sunlight.

However after the Second World War house plants are becoming more and more popular. More and more facilities are becoming available to favour this hobby.

More cultivars which need direct sunlight for a long time of the day can be grown in the front yard, verandah, window sills and on roof terraces. As they are grown in pots at the flowering stage they can be shifted inside the room with advantage for the enjoyment of perfume.

The following species and cultivars which bear fragrant flowers can be grown indoors:

Trees:	*Gardenia latifolia, Magnolia fuscata, M. mutabilis, M. pumila, Michelia alba, Nyctanthes arbor-tristis, Plumeria spcs.*
Shrubs:	*Cestrum nocturnum, Gardenia spcs., Ixora parviflora, Jasminum officinale, J. auriculatum, J. sambac, Murraya paniculata.*
Climbers:	*Clematis fammula.*
Bulbous plants:	*Eucaris grandiflora, Hedychium coronarium, Lilium* spcs., Orchid spcs., Tuberose.
Annual herbs:	Alyssum, Carnation, Nicotiana, Sweet pea, Sweet sultan, Reseda.

Where to Grow

The plants bearing fragrant flowers, unlike foliage plants, need more light. Both duration and intensity should be lengthy and high. Hence they can hardly be grown in diffused light exclusively. So for them we need a place lighted by the direct sun for at least six hours a day. Hence roof terrace and patio are suitable for growing these plants. During the period of flowering they can be brought indoors and placed in a position having more light, diffused or direct.

How to Grow

For changing position it is convenient to grow plants in pots. In a dry and hot summer the delicate plants need protection against hot wind and western sun. The plants, if potted, can be shifted to the suitable position conveniently.

For growing plants in pots suitable potting compost and pots are required, the details of potting compost and potting operation have been dealt with already.

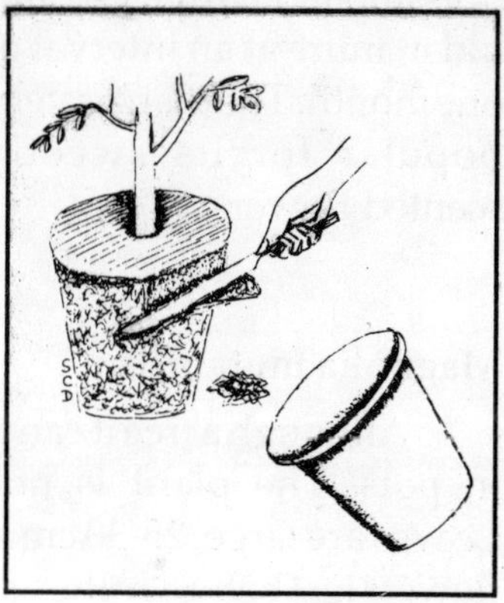

ROOT PRUNING

Root Pruning: The old pot plants usually need root pruning. Just in the beginning of monsoon the plant with its soil ball will be taken out of the pot. After pruning its roots as shown in the diagram the plant will be potted again as usual.

Gardenia latifolia

It is a tree and hardly found in gardens. But it can be grown in pots. It bears very fragrant flowers in April-May. The plant is propagated by air layering or seeds. It, unlike other gardenias, bears plenty of fruits. Seeds are small, which germinate within four weeks of sowing.

Although a tree it can be grown in pots. The plants obtained by layering are suitable for pot culture.

Magnolia fuscata

It is a dwarf magnolia which grows well in pots. Moreover the plant is very shade-loving, which thrives even in the absence of direct sunlight. It hardly exceeds one metre in height. Leaves, like camellia, are small and glossy. Flowers are small (3 cm across) yellowish green with a brown-purple flush and fragrance. It is propagated by layering (air or ground).

M. fuscata flowers from March to October. Apply top dressing in February or liquid manure at an interval of one month. The plant is very popular for its sweetly scented flowers.

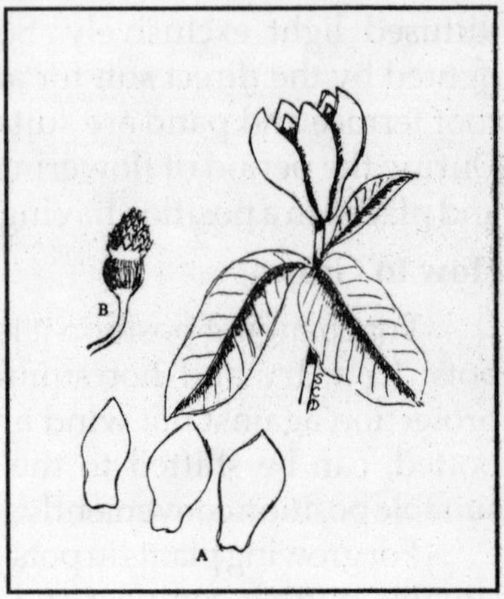

MAGNOLIA FUSCATA
A. Petals
B. Stamens and Carpels

Magnolia mutabilis

Although a tree it can be grown in pots. The plant is not bushy. Leaves are large, 25-30 cm long. The flowers just before anthesis look like a duck egg of golden colour.

The plants propagated by air layering are grown in pots. *M. mutabilis* is a shade-loving plant which grows well in a semi-shade position. It responds well to general cultural operations.

MAGNOLIA MUTABILIS
Branch with a Bud (just before Anthesis)

Magnolia pumila

An evergreen bushy plant of hot and humid area. The elliptic leaves are narrowed at both ends. Flowers are creamy white, very fragrant and covered with petal-like waxy green sepals which are white inside. Flowers open in the evening and emit perfume only for 15-20 minutes. It like, *M. fuscata*, thrives in a shady place. Hence a good indoor plant.

Michelia alba

The plant is very popular for its white scented flowers which are available almost throughout the year. In the plains it hardly sets seeds. Hence it is propagated by grafting. The seedling of *M. champaca* is used as a rootstock for grafting.

The plant grows well in pots. It responds readily to manuring in form of top dressing or liquid manure. The plant needs pruning at an interval of 2-3 years. When a plant becomes pot-bound it needs root pruning.

Nyctanthes arbor-tristis

Although a tree it is usually grown as a shrub. In a pot the plant can be grown as a small shrub. The plant is propagated by seeds or air layering. Sow few seeds in a pot in April. Select only the healthy seedling and destroy the rest. When 10 cm high pinch the top to force side branches. Nyctanthes is a quick growing plant and responds well to manuring. It flowers from June-October. The plant should be pruned in November. Half of the height should be removed while pruning. Heading back the flowering shoots when flowering of the particular shoot is over is also necessary.

Plumeria

Very few species of Plumeria are grown as a pot plant. A variety named 'Apurva' which was developed by the author is extremely floriferous. It flowers well even in pots. A few cultivars have been imported recently that flower well in pots.

Plumeria is propagated by cuttings. It needs less manure and water.

Cestrum nocturnum

C. nocturnum is propagated by cuttings or clump divisions. It is a very quick growing plant and responds well to general cultural operations. It needs pruning and top dressing at the end of winter.

Gardenia

All species and varieties of gardenia are successfully

grown in pots. The plants should be protected from the western sun and hot wind in summer. They flower in summer and the rains. The plants are propagated by air layering or cuttings.

Ixora parviflora

It is a tall shrub but in pots it becomes dwarf. It is a very hardy plant which responds to manuring quickly. It should be grown in a heavy compost. Because in a light compost the plant sends out plenty of suckers.

The plant is propagated by suckers or air layering. It hardly needs pruning. But at an interval of few years root pruning may be necessary.

Jasminum officinale

This species is very hardy and its culture is easier than that of all other jasmines. Though a good climber it can be grown as a dwarf shrub in pots. If the pot is placed close to a verandah grill or fence netting it climbs up well as on a trellis.

The plant is propagated by cuttings or ground layering. It, like other jasmines, needs pruning in February. Before setting seeds the spent up flowering shoots should be removed.

Jasminum sambac

It is an ideal pot plant. The plant is propagated easily by cuttings. The plants respond well to manuring. Prune the plant in February and apply a good top dressing.

Jasminum auriculatum

Its culture is same as that of *J. officinale*.

Murraya paniculata

It can be a good pot plant. The plant is highly ornamental with beautiful dark green glossy foliage. The plant is propagated by seed or air layering. Murraya flowers from summer to autumn. It hardly needs pruning. But root pruning becomes necessary at an interval of a few years.

Eucharis grandiflora

It is a good bulbous plant, which prefers hilly region and moist climate and responds well in a semi-shade condition. Eucharis grows better in a pot. It, like amaryllis, should be left for a long time, say, 4-8 years. It needs a very rich compost. Feed supplements should be applied twice or thrice a year.

The plant is propagated by bulbs which are planted in February. In a large pot three bulbs can be planted 20 cm apart.

Hedychium coronarium

It is a rhizomatous plant which flowers from March to October. The plant is propagated by roots or seeds. Each plant has one flowering shoot. A bunch bears a good number of flowers. When flowering is over the green portion of the plant is removed. Then new shoots come up from the roots. At an interval of three years replanting may be necessary.

Hedychium needs hot and humid surroundings. So it needs more watering in summer.

Lilium

It is a bulbous plant which grows well in pots. One bulb is planted in a pot with good compost. Although a long stemmed plant it becomes short when grown in pots. No feeding is required in winter. One top dressing and four dosages of liquid manure are usually required. The top dressing should be applied in February and the liquid manure at an interval of two months.

Orchid

Orchids are grown in pots with a special type of compost which is devoid of soil. See 'Gardening with Fragrant Flowers'.

Tuberose (*Polyanthes tuberosa*)

One of the most popular flowers for indoor gardening. It is a bulbous plant which can be grown easily in a pot. In a 30 cm pot three bulbs are planted 20 cm apart. The pot soil should be heavy with clay. Because tuberose does not prefer a light soil. Flowering is much less in a soil that cannot retain moisture and nutrients. A fine-textured soil, unlike sandy soil, does not run dry quickly and not only that, the plant food cannot leach out easily through it. Food supplements have to be applied at an interval of 6-8 weeks. Replanting with large bulbs should be done every year in February-April.

Alyssum

A beautiful annual of white flowers, which is highly suitable for hanging baskets. Alyssum flowers within 6 weeks of sowing seeds. It is better to sow seeds directly in the pots in which it will flower. Thin out the seedlings keeping few at a distance of 7-10 cm.

Carnation (*Dianthus caryophyllus*)

In our sub-tropical climate carnation is grown as a winter annual. It is mostly grown in pots. For agro-technique see 'Commercial Culture of Fragrant Flowers'.

Nicotiana (*N. alata*)

It is a winter annual. In the plains seeds are sown in September to November. Generally one-month-old seedlings are transplanted in pots. 3-4 seedlings are grown in a pot.

Sweet Sultan (*Centaurea moschata*)

It is an annual herb grown in winter. Generally it is grown in ground. But it can also be grown in pots. The plant is propagated by seeds. In a 30 cm pot 3 plants can be grown. 2-3 week old seedlings are transplanted in pots. Flowering takes place within 12 weeks of sowing.

Sweet Pea (*Lathyrus odorata*)

It is a seasonal flower, mostly climbing and grown in ground. But dwarf varieties have been introduced which are better for pot culture. The tall varieties need support for climbing. But by inserting long stakes in pots or placing the pot close to a fence netting the tall varieties can be grown.

Sweet pea is propagated by seeds which are sown in October in the plains. In a 30 cm pot 3 plants of tall varieties or 6 plants of dwarf varieties can be grown. Sweet pea needs less nitrogen and more other nutrients. Seed pods should be removed or flowering will be reduced.

Reseda

It is an ideal annual for pot culture. Usually it is grown in pots rather than in ground. The plant is bushy. Long compact flower spikes above the green foliage look very beautiful.

Sow few seeds in a pot and thin out the seedlings keeping only three per pot. After sowing press the seeds on the compost which facilitates quick germination. Reseda grows best in a light potting compost. Although moisture loving it should be grown in a well-drained soil in a sunny situation. Hence care should be taken to crock the drain hole properly and the pots be kept at the most sunny place of the garden.

Clematis (*C. fammula*)

It is a good plant for growing in pots. Though a heavy climber it can be grown as a bushy shrub in pots. It is also grown as a climber if the pots are placed close to a verandah grill or fence netting.

Clematis flowers through the rains. The plant is propagated by clump division or ground layering. On certain places it produces seeds.

GARDENING WITH FRAGRANT FLOWERS

TREES

Albizzia lebbek

Local names: Sans. & Mar.—Sirisha; Hindi—Siris; Beng.—Sirish; Guj. — Pilo Sarshio; Tel.—Dirasana; Tam.—Vagei; Kan.—Bagemara; Mal.—Vaga; Burma—Kikko

It is a common and very popular tree of Eastern India. The plant itself is ornamental and with fragrant flowers in spring is extremely beautiful and overpowering. The mass of greenish white flowers against the background of light green tender foliage looks nice. The tree trunk is straw yellow hence the name 'yellow *siris*'.

The plant is propagated from seeds. It is grown as an avenue tree. Its timber is valuable for furniture.

Alstonia scholaris

Local names: Sans.—Saptaparna; Hindi—Chatian; Beng.—Chattim; Mar.—Satvin; Tam. & Mal.—Pala; Kan.—Maddale

The plant grows wild and is also planted along the roadsides. It is a very tall tree which may grow to a height of 24 metres or more. Leaves are very glossy and beautifully arranged in a whorl of 5-7 forming a bunch.

Alstonia blooms from October-December when the pollens with perfume fill the surrounding air. Its pollen, however, causes air pollution. People having asthmatic trouble may feel uncomfortable while inhaling the air abounding in its pollen.

Alstonia is propagated from seeds or cuttings. The air layering is also practised. As the seeds are very thin and dispersed very quickly by air care should be taken to collect the fruits just before ripening, i.e., the mature pods should be picked before splitting.

The seeds germinate early on sowing and the seedlings grow fast.

Anthocephalus indicus

Local names: Sans., Hindi, Beng., Mar. and Guj. Kadamba; Tel.—Kadambama; Tam.—Vellai cadamba; Kan.—Kadawala; Mal.—Attutek; Burma—Mau-le-ttanshe

Kadamba is a very popular tree for its beautiful fragrant flowers, pleasant shade and fine-grained timber. A fast-growing large deciduous tree with a straight stem of about

10 m height. In a rich soil no tree can be so fast-growing as Kadamba. The seedling can attain 2.5 m height in the first year. The rounded crown with large leaves casts a very pleasant shade. The plant flowers in the beginning of the rainy season and perfumes the air all around.

The plant is propagated by seed on sowing in seed pans during April-June. The seeds are dispersed by air when capsules burst. So the mature heads should be collected in time. Winter being the proper time for collecting heads for seed. Seeds sown on fine compost germinate well during the hot months. Although the seeds are minute seedlings become conspicuous quickly. If a rich compost is used in the seed pan seedlings grow very fast.

Kadamba is considered a good planting material for avenues and parks as well as large gardens. It is also commonly found in the temple and school premises. The *Brahma Vaivarta Purana* says: "Planting of Kadamba brings only good to a village."

Citrus aurantium

Local names: Hindi—Khatta; Tam.—Narayan, Narattai; Tel.—Mallika narangi; Kan.—Heraly; Mal.—Karna

In home gardens *Jambheri* (*C. aurantium*) is grown from seed as it breeds almost true. To avoid variation through seed propagation grafting (budding) should be done onto the rootstock of any sour orange taking scion from a selected floriferous variety. See 'Field culture for perfumery industry' for details of culture.

Coroupita guianensis

Local names: Nagalingam, Nagachampa, Nageswarar Champa, Sivalingam

The tree with its unique appearance is a great attraction especially in the botanical gardens of India. The plant bears many long woody flower bunches laden with buds, flowers and large ball-like fruits through all seasons of the year. Although the flowering time is the hot months the old trees bear flowers throughout the year. The coroupita bears large unique fleshy flowers in a combination of rosy, purple, white and yellow petals on the trunk of a tree.

The tree is a native of tropical south Africa and was introduced into Ceylon (now Sri Lanka) in 1881. It flowered for the first time in 1898 (Macmillan—Tropical Planting and Gardening).

The cultivation of the plant is not so widespread as it deserves. Scarcity of the planting materials is said to be one of the reasons. Another reason is that it does not flower until the plant becomes 10-15 years of age. But once flowered it remains currous for a century or so. A typical flower bunch is found to hold large fruits, fragrant flowers and buds of different sizes at the same time. Another unique feature is that the plant sheds its leaves completely twice or thrice a year. The new leaves, however, cover the tree shortly after defoliation.

The plant is propagated by seeds which germinate satisfactorily. Coroupita is a quick growing plant that thrives in a moist climate.

Gardenia latifolia

Local names: Hindi—Papra, Paphar; Beng.—Pindalu; Mar.—Ghogri; Tel.—Pedda bikki; Tam.—Kumbay; Kan.—Kalkambi; Oriya—Kota ranga

Although the tree is covered with large fragrant flowers *G. latifolia* is still a tree of the forest. Because you will hardly come across it in a garden. It is an ideal tree for parks and avenues. During April-May the plant is covered with large white fragrant flowers. The stale flowers becomes yellowish. The tree bears plenty of fruits which ripen in September. The fruit is compact with small hard seeds resembling those of guava.

Sow the seeds from April-June, very small percentage of seeds will germinate. The growth of seedlings is very slow. The leaves at the seedling stage form a rosette as the internodes are very short or absent. A young plant takes 4-5 years for flowering. As it grows wild the plant does not demand any special care. But goats are very fond of its foliage and bark. So it needs protection from browsing.

Madhuca indica (Syn. *Bassia latifolia*)

Local names: Hindi—Mahua, Mohwa, Manwa; Beng.—Mahwa, Maul, Mahula; Mar.—Mahwa, Mahwra; Guj.—Mahuda, Tel.—Ippa; Tam.—Illupei; Kan.—Hippe; Mal.—Poonam; Oriya—Mahula, Madgi

Mahua can stand drought and frost to a great extent. It can be grown in various soils and climates. It is found even in water-logged or low-lying clay and shallow soil in Karnataka. The plant can also stand excessive monsoon and demands strong direct sunlight. It flowers in spring. The fragrant flowers that look like large (2 cm across) translucent beads are a great attraction. Flowers are fleshy, juicy, bead-like, translucent and strongly scented. Dry flowers that look like raisin are used in preparing country wine.

Mahua is propagated by seed. In nature most of them dispersed in the forest are destroyed by insects and pests. Only those which are covered (soon after dispersal) with earth or debris raise their sprout early in the rains. The seedlings which get sufficient sunlight may survive.

In nursery seedlings can be raised by sowing seeds in depth. June-July is a suitable period for sowing. Seeds in beds or pans must be covered with compost. The seedlings must be provided with sufficient direct sun. The long tap-root of *Mahua* seedlings poses a problem for safe transplanting. So seedlings raised in deep pots or sowing in the site (*in situ*) being the usual practice.

The flowers collected and dried form an important article of food both for men and animals in central India and yield by distillation a country spirit. The seeds yield an inferior oil, largely eaten by the tribal people.

Magnolia grandiflora

Local names: Hindi—Anda champa, Him champa; Beng.—Jojangandha

The plant is very popular in West Bengal. Although its flowering is regular only in the district of Darjeeling the people in the plains near Calcutta are found to be fanatical for its inclusion into their gardens. The soil near Calcutta, unlike the Southern States, is suitable for its growth and flowering only in the gardens with rich alluvium. The plant grows normally to a height of 3-5 metres near Calcutta. It flowers once in a year, which is in April.

The flowers are creamy white to white in colour and stand upright in the form of a cup, 15-20 cm across. The size of the flowers is, however, smaller in plains than that found in Loyd Botanical Garden at Darjeeling. Secondly the sexual parts, stamens and carpels, grow at the cost of the sepals and petals; still the seed setting is rare.

Propagation of the plant by air layering is in vogue. Grafting onto the rootstocks of other species of magnolia will be suitable for the plains. For raising a beautiful plant the selection of stocks is in practice. So it should be propagated from a plant that has attained a good height and regular flowering habit.

For better growth and flowering manurial practice should be regularly attended to. Balanced manuring with farmyard manure, oil cake, super phosphate and potassic fertilizers during October/November stimulates good flowering in the gardens near Calcutta. Pruning is not generally required except for the dead wood.

Magnolia fuscata

See 'Indoor Gardening'.

Magnolia mutabilis

Local names: Beng.—Jahuri champa

See 'Indoor Gardening'.

Magnolia pterocarpa

Local names: Beng.—Dulichampa; Nepal—Pat pate; Assam—Thouthou; Baramp thuri-sopa; Lakhimpur—Balomturi

It is a tall evergreen shade-loving tree which thrives in a moist climate. The direct sun and hot wind in summer cause leaf scorch leading to the death of the plant.

Seed setting is rare, so propagation by ground layering is in practice. Grafting on suitable rootstocks may be tried. Flowers with six fleshy petals are 6-9 cm across, which bloom in April-May.

In dry areas it should be grown in shade, and in summer it should be provided with adequate moisture. Moreover the plant must be protected from the hot wind.

Magnolia Pumila

See 'Indoor Gardening'.

Mesua ferrea

Local names: Hindi & Beng.—Nagkesar, Nageswar; Guj. & Mar.—Nagachampa, Tel.—Nagkesara; Tam.—Nangu, Kan.—Nagkesara; Mal.—Nanga; Assamese—Nahor

Mesua ferrea does well in the foothills of Eastern India. It is an excellent tree favoured much for its graceful appearance, attractive tender foliage and large fragrant flowers. Flowers are about 6 cm across and look like a magnolia. They are strongly fragrant and white in colour.

It prefers a moist climate and porous soil. In the plains the mortality of young plants that usually occurs is troublesome. The plant is propagated by seed. When transplanting the position of the plants should be lowered by 50 cm from the surface level. On the occasion of hot spell during summer the young plants should preferably be protected from sun by providing shade. The plant is slow growing especially in the plains. Secondly it, like *Coroupita guianensis,* takes a long time to flower. Not only that it also sheds leaves more than once a year.

Michelia champaca

Local names: Hindi—Champa, Champaka; Beng.—Swarna champa; Mar.—Pivala-champa, Sona champa, Kud-Champa; Guj.—Champo, Pito champo; Tel.—Champa, Kanu; Tam.—Shembuga; Kan.—Samige, Mal.—Champakam; Oriya—Chompa, Chompoko; Nepali—Oulia champ; Assamese—Tilasopa

Although it grows to a clean cylindrical trunk upto 50 m high in forests but a handsome tree of medium height in gardens. It is considered one of the giant trees of India. The specimens found in the forests of Kollegal division of Karnataka and Mayurbhanj of Orissa are to surpass all giants by having a height of 64 m and girth of 20.35 m at the breast height.

Champaka is a favourite plant of Indian gardens. The flowering is due twice a year—once in spring and other in autumn; practically however it extends from March to October. In very old trees a few flowers can be seen any time in winter. A young plant takes 4-6 years for flowering. Trees usually bear profuse seeds after flowering. If they are allowed to mature the flowering in the following season will invariably be reduced. So be wise to remove the bunches of fruits early. Spring seeds ripen in autumn when they are immediately collected for sowing. The viability of seed is very short (a few weeks only). Secondly the germination is not regular as the seed coat is very hard. Rubbing off the hard seed coat on a rough surface before sowing is in practice. Seeds sown during July-September germinate well. On the contrary, winter sowing hardly gives any good result.

Seeds should be sown in a good compost in seed pans. Watering must be regular. The seedlings of 7-10 cm in height are transferred to 20 cm pots. The seedlings when sufficiently large in the pot should be planted in ground at the beginning of the rains. The seedlings grow better in moderate shade.

Champaka prefers sandy loam and moist climate. Young plants suffer most in a hot dry atmosphere. In an arid zone care should be taken to select a suitable site for planting. It should preferably be near other garden trees or buildings. The mortality due to dry hot weather in summer does not occur to the plants growing close to a building. The plants already planted away from such things may be provided the similar effect by paving around the plant with stones or bricks. 15-20 sq m area covered under pavement is sufficient for a tree.

It requires manuring as applied to an average fruit tree for good growth and heavy bearing. Pruning is not necessary except for the removal of dead wood. If necessary a plant can be pruned in June (see pruning). Nurserymen propagate champaka by grafting also for early flowering. The rootstocks used being the seedlings of the same species. The grafts are grown in pots and brought indoors when in bloom. This can be a fond fancy for the fragrant fanciers. Inarching being the usual practice for grafting. Patch budding, however, may be tried in early spring.

Michelia alba

Local name: Swet champa

In *M. alba* seed setting is rare. For this reason it is propagated by grafting onto the seedling of *M. champaca.* Its grafts can be a good pot plant, and highly ornamental with profuse flowers. The flowering period of *M. alba* is much longer than *champaka,* which extends as long as ten months a year. It, unlike *M. champaca,* thrives in an ordinary condition. Because it is hardy and vigorous.

Millingtonia hortensis

Local names: Hindi—Mini chameli; Beng.—Akasnim; Mar.—Akas-nimb; Tel.—Kavuki; Tam.—Mara-malli; Kan.—Beratu; Mal.—Katesam; Oriya—Bakeni, Mach-mach, Sitahara

By virtue of its stately form, ornamental foliage and profusion of perfumed flowers *M. hortensis* has got preference in gardens, parks and avenues. It flowers twice a year. The spent flowers drop and make a white carpet beneath.

An evergreen tree of straight elongated and pyramidal form grows up to 25 m in height. The leaves are ornamental, which resemble those of *neem*. The flower bunches are pendulous and terminal.

In moist areas it seldom sets seeds. So its propagation is done by means of root suckers which grow in abundance about the tree. The heavy suckering habit makes it unsuitable for a small garden. The viability of seeds is very low. So they should be sown immediately after the fruit has ripened. It can also be propagated by cuttings. The wood is brittle and liable to be snapped off by strong winds.

Mimusops elengi

Local names: Hindi—Maulsarai; Beng.—Bakul; Mar.—Ovalli; Guj.—Barsoli, Bolsari; Tel.—Pagode; Tam.—Vagulam, Magadam; Kan.—Bakula, Pagode; Mal.—Elengi, Ilanni; Oriya—Bakula baula; Assamese—Gokul

This is a large evergreen tree of rounded head with thick branching and dense foliage. Leaves are 8-14 cm long with wavy edges. The flowers are dull white, star-shaped and sweetly scented. They open after evening and drop before daybreak.

The tree usually attains large dimensions in moist climate and sandy soil. It is usually propagated by seed. The ripe fruits are liked by birds that cause the seed dispersal. Seeds germinate well in the shady nook of the grove or forest.

Seedlings can also be raised in nursery. For good germination the pans should be placed in the most shady corner of the garden. It takes few weeks to germinate. Seeds should be sown in April/May. The seedlings grow well in a rich soil. Although the growth is slow, practically it continues through all seasons. A plant requires 5-6 years of growth to flower. *Maulsarai* is an excellent shade tree which is very popular for growing in parks, avenues and home gardens.

Maulsarai is susceptibe to fungous attack. The infection starts at the cut end. The heartwood of the affected tree is destroyed thereby making a hollow along the pith. Any suitable fungicide should be applied at the cut end. Copper fungicides like Blitox, Bordeaux mixture, etc. are quite effective. Borer Weevils make holes on the trunk and penetrate the wood. It can be controlled by applying kerosene oil into the hole and sealing the opening by wax.

Mitragyna parviflora

Local names: Hindi—Koem; Beng.—Gulikadam; Tam.—Chinnakadam, Kan.—Kongu; Mal.—Vimbu; Oriya—Gudikaima

It is an ideal tree for gardens and avenues. Unfortunately it is found mostly in forests. Hence its importance is more as a timber tree than as a flowering plant. In many aspects it is very close to *Kadamba (A. indicus).* But the flowering time and the size of the flower head differ.

The diameter of a flower head is just the half of *Kadamba.* The flowering period being spring-summer. Size and shape of the tree and flowering time vary. As it is summer flowering the tree is not clothed with foliage at the time of flowering. Though the size of the flower head is small the quantity of flowers per tree is much more than that of *Kadamba.*

During its flowering *M. parviflora* is really enchanting with its sweetly scented flowers. The seeds are very minute. The collection of seeds and raising seedlings are same as those of *Kadamba.*

Plumeria

Local names: Sans.—Khira Champa; Hindi—Gul-e-chin; Assamese—Galanchi; Beng.—Katchampa, Golan champa, Garur champa; Kan.—Kadusampage; Guj.—Dhola champo; Mal.—Arali; Mar.—Khair champa; Tam.—Perungali; Tel.—Arhataganneru; Oriya—Golochi; Santal—Champa pungar, Gularjbaha

The name 'Plumeria' is after the distinguished French priest, traveller and botanist Charles Plumer (1664-1706). The plant is very hardy and grows vigorously without any difficulty. Hence known as a 'Symbol of Health'. Plumerias are noted for their sweet perfume. Its stems and leaves have a very thick milky latex. Hence, its name 'Frangipani' which means 'coagulating milk' in French.

Growing plumerias is very easy. They are grown in gardens and parks, in avenues and temple premises. It is also commonly found in burial grounds. Plumerias are easily multiplied by seeds and stem cuttings. Most of the varieties are propagated by cuttings that root well in summer. On account of its semi-succulent nature the fleshy bark may rot in excess moisture before rooting. Hence the success is more if tried during the dry months. A good practice is this: cut a stem more than 60 cm in length in November. Place in the shade in a dry condition, preferably covered with dry sand. In the month of February it should be planted out when callus has been formed at the cut end. Another method which is termed as 'callusing' and etiolating' is very effective for the difficult-to-root species. Make a griddle 25 mm wide by removing the bark at the base of the portion of the shoot to be used as cutting. The treated shoot should not be detached from the plant until callus is formed at the cut end. For causing etiolation the base of the cutting should be wrapped with a strip of black polythene so that the chlorophyll of the covered portion is destroyed due to the absence of sunlight.

P. acutifolia

See Plumeria in Chapter 1.

P. alba

See Plumeria in Chapter 1.

P. rubra

See Plumeria in Chapter 1.

Pterospermum acerefolium

Local names: Hindi—Kainar; Beng.—Kanakchampa, Muchkunda; Tel.—Matsa Kanda; Oriya—Kanaka champa

It is a large attractive evergreen tree of dark green foliage. Leaves are rounded (about 20 cm across). The upper surface is dark green and the lower silvery. The flowers that look like a half peeled banana are 12-15 cm long with five fleshy sepals and five white membranous petals. Its strongly fragrant flowers appear solitarily in the leaf axils from April-June.

The plant is propagated by seeds and cuttings. For vegetative propagation soft-wood cuttings should be used. It is grown in parks, gardens and avenues.

Nyctanthes arbor-tristis

Local names: Sans.—Parijat, Sephalika; Hindi—Hara singar, Seoli; Beng.—Sephalika, Seoli; Mar.—Khurasli, Parijatak; Guj.—Jayaparvati; Tel.—Pagadamelle, Parijatamu; Tam.—Manijhapu; Kan.—Harsing, Parijata; Mal.—Parijatokom; Oriya—Godokodiko, Singaroharo; Mundari — Saparom

The plant is widely cultivated in the gardens of India for its fragrant flowers. It is easily propagated by seeds and cuttings. It hardly requires any manuring in an average soil. Seedlings raised in April are transplanted in May/June. In a rich soil it grows to a height of 2 m by August and flowering may start in September/October of the same year. The rooted cuttings grown in pots also give flowers. Clonal propagation by cutting or grafting becomes necessary to perpetuate the desirable variations selected from a large plant population. The workers of the National Botanical Research Institute (Lucknow) have found a range of variations in the size and shape of flowers, the extent of flower opening and corolla tubes by their critical observation. They have made a number of interesting selections which are being propagated by budding (Srivastava, 1976).

SHRUBS

Cestrum nocturnum

Local names: Beng.—Hasu-na-hana

The plant is highly prized for its strongly fragrant flowers. It blooms after evening and makes a pleasant environment all around with sweet fragrance.

Generally the plants are grown near verandahs or windows to enjoy sweet smell over the whole night. A close planting in a row makes a good hedge in the garden.

Stem cuttings (25 cm long) or layering is the normal method of propagation. Semi-hard cuttings root easily. They should be treated with a fungicide before putting into the sand medium. The cut end (lower) of the branches may be treated with root-hormone powder for a good root formation. All cuttings are found to root if not destroyed by any fungal attack. The rooted cuttings in the early stage should not be planted directly in ground. Each cutting with its good root system should be planted in a 15 cm pot with good potting compost and should be kept in shade for a week or so for curing.

Hasu-na-hana gives a good response to manuring. The application of farmyard manure, oil cake and *suphala* makes the shrub quick growing. Manure should be applied in the pit before planting and once a year after pruning in February as a top dressing. Hard pruning may, however, be necessitated once in a few years' interval.

As the branches are slender and week a support is usually required against lodging; but staking with poles is unsightly. A roll of welded-wire or woven-wire mesh erected round the plant like a fencing will give a good support without impairing the appearance rather it will help form a uniform and balanced growth of the bush. Secondly this will protect the plant from strong winds. If the base of the plant is shaken by storm the plant is likely to die.

Cestrum cannot stand water-logging, so good drainage is essential. The life of the bush is shortened in a soil of bad drainage. Wilting is one of the serious diseases that kills the bush. It is caused due to harmful soil fungi. In order to prevent wilting grafting may be tried on the rootstocks (other species of this genus, say, *N. diurnum, N. parqui,* etc.).

Gardenia

Local names: Beng.—Gandharaj

The plant is named in honour of Dr. Alexander Garden,

an 18th century botanist from South Carolina. The gardenia is noted for its fragrant flowers. Ranging from dwarf to a large sized bushy shrub reaching a height of 1-3 metres. Its flowers are solitary, white, single, semi-double or double and strongly fragrant. They appear from spring to the rains. Gardenia does not set seed in our climate. The cultivars are widely grown in all parts of India. They are considered very interesting subjects of home gardens. Gardenias grow well in a partially shady place. They should be protected from western sun and hot wind.

Manures and fertilizers may be applied for better flowering. Phosphatic fertilizers in form of super phosphate, bonemeal should be applied during the rains. A mixture of following ingredients is sufficient for a standard plant for yearly application:

Cow-manure	5 litres
Urea	50 grams
Super phosphate	75 grams
Muriate of potash	50 grams
Magnesium sulphate	10 grams

The plant is propagated by cuttings or air layering. In certain regions any variety may suffer from root gall disease. This can be remedied by grafting the susceptible variety onto the rootstock of another variety which is resistant to this disease.

Gardenia florida var Fortunei: A bushy shrub that bears beautiful double flowers of 8 cm across. The flowers are white, well formed and strongly scented.

G. florida var Veitchii: It is a dwarf species. A very well formed compact bush. It has flowers that are small but well formed resembling a white rose. The plant often suffers from the root gall disease and consequently the bud drop becomes a perennial trouble. This can be remedied by grafting it onto the rootstocks of other species of gardenia, say, *G. fortunei*, *G. lucida* or *G. florida*.

G. kirkii: It bears star-shaped single flowers. The leaves are dark green.

G. lucida: It is a large shrub or small tree. The flowers are white and scented. They last for a few days and turn yellow on ageing.

Ixora parviflora

Local names: Beng.—Swet Rangan

It is a tall shrub of white fragrant flowers. *I. parviflora* is the tallest species of the genus (*Ixora*). Sometimes it looks like a dwarf tree. The plant is very hardy that hardly needs any care as demanded by other garden plantation. Its propagation is so easy that it can be compared with that of a weed. Because the plant sends out numerous suckers around the plant especially in a light soil. Propagation by suckers is easier than making air layering or marcottage.

The plant flowers in summer. The mass of white fragrant flowers covers the plant when every shoot terminates with a large bunch of flowers.

Jasmine

A Latinised version of the Arabic name *yasmin*. It is a very large family comprising numerous species and varieties distributed all over the world. It grows in tropical, subtropical and temperate regions. The plants are shrubs or climbers or in between. Jasmines are valued much for their strongly fragrant flowers in home gardens, cut-flower trade and perfumery. It is also true that all jasmines are not strongly fragrant nor that all of them are cultivated species. Many of them are also found to grow in their wild habitat. The wild ones are mostly fragrant but not so attractive and floriferous as the cultivated. Although the name 'Jasmine' fills one's mind with the profusion of white fragrant flowers but there are few yellow varieties which are the variations. They are mildly perfumed and less floriferous.

There is no Indian garden without a jasmine as no European garden without a rose. The place of jasmines in our gardens is same as it was in ancient times. It is worth mentioning that the advent of the numerous exotic flowers in our gardens has not been able to fade the fervour for the jasmine. To enjoy the sweet fragrance from a close proximity we plant jasmines near the windows, verandahs and train them to climb up the trellis on the roof terraces.

Jasmines flower in hot months but there are few which prefer cold weather for flowering. The latter are hardly fragrant. Other than jasmine we have many scented flowers in our gardens but jasmines are more popular and universal for the reasons that need no explanation.

Jasmines grow in a wide range of climates from the tropical to the temperate. Not only in the plains they are found to grow on hills upto 3,000 m also. They are widely distributed all over India. Numerous varieties under forty species are recorded. The varieties are mostly horticultural selections based on the economic importance. Among them *J. auriculatum, J. officinale* (including *'forma grandiflora'*) and *J. sambac* are commercially important as the sources of flowers for fresh flower trade or perfumery. There are others which produce showy flowers but less fragrant. They are extremely hardy and grown in home gardens. Those species are *J. arborescens, J. malabaricum, J. multiflorum,* etc.

Jasminum grandiflorum

Local names: Sans.—Chambeli, Chetaki, Jati, Malati; Hindi & Beng.—Chameli, Jati; Guj.— Chambili; Tel.—Jaji, Malligai, Pichi; Mal.—Pichikam, Pichakāmulla; Kan.—Ajjige, Jaji, Mallige, Jati mallige; Punjabi—Chamba, Chambeli

In home gardens chameli is grown from cuttings. For highly ornamental leaves and strongly fragrant flowers it is liked by many. But it is not so hardy as other jasmines. Therefore care should be taken to protect the plants from pests and diseases. Leafspot (a fungous disease) and root gall are the common trouble. For remedy see 'the field culture of fragrant flowers for perfumery industry'. The cultural details are same as those of *J. officinale.*

Jasminum officinale

Local names: Jui, Chameli

It is a very beautiful climbing shrub with highly ornamental shining leaves. It blooms from April to November. Being self-climbing it reaches 6 m height on support. For its delightful scented flowers *J. officinale* is very common in home gardens. The plant is propagated by layers or suckers. The stem cuttings also root well. It demands a rich soil and for this reason responds well to manuring. Manures and fertilizers should be applied after pruning in spring. Light pruning is usually required to remove unwanted growths and spent up flowering shoots. Sucker growths must be suppressed or flowering will decrease. No special treatment is usually required for pests and diseases that hardly create any problem.

Jasminum sambac

Local names: Sans.—Mallika; Hindi—Banamallika, Chamba, Mogra; Beng.—Motia, Mogra, Bel, Beli, Bela; Mar.—Mogra, But mogra; Tel.-Boddumalla, Gundumalle; Tam.—Adukkumalli, Gundumalli; Kan.—Elusutter malliga, Mar.—Cheru pichakam, Kudamulla

Different cultivars:

i) *Matiya* (Tam.—Virupakshi)—Globular buds, double flowers with rounded petals.
ii) *Bela* (Tam.—Gundumalli)—Double-flowered with elongated petals.
iii) *Maturia*—Semi-double flowers.
iv) *Hazara bela* (Kan.—Suji mallige)—Flowers single.
v) *Mogra* (Tam.—Adukkumalli)—Full double, button-flowered type. The bud is 25 mm in diam. One form of which is creamy white and known as Grand Duke of Tascany. Mogra sometimes passes as *J. trifoliatum*.
vi) *Madanwan* (Beng.—Madanban)—Unlike others its bud is long and pointed, which opens suddenly, as if by a spring action.

For its floriferous habit and strongly scented flowers sambac is a popular item in home gardens. According to the botanists, there are several thousand species of flowering plants in Philippine. But the queen of the Philippine flowers and the national flower is that "Sampaguita" (*J. sambac*). To them it is a symbol of love, youth and friendship. According to their tradition, a youngman who is too timid to express his love to a girl may send her a sambac garland, especially on the eve of a dance. If she wears it he finds reason to long for her.

The plant is propagated by cuttings. Suckers or layers are taken from those (especially Mogras) which are not easily multiplied by stem cuttings. Such varieties should be fertilized in an optimum dose, as a result of which a good number of basal shoots will come up. Some of them will run horizontally above the ground forming roots at the nodes like runners. Now plants can be grown from the divisions of runner shoots.

J. sambac blooms over a long period from March to October in the plains. In order to force early flowering prune the bushes at the height of 60 cm in late winter, and apply manures and fertilizers liberally. The forcing must be preceded by a dry condition to make the bushes dormant. It becomes perfect for heavy blossoms if the plants are denuded of leaves or the leaves retained are stripped off at the time of pruning.

The frequency of irrigation is determined by the growth of shoots and flower buds. Until flower buds appear irrigation should be normal, then it is increased to provide more moisture for rapid growth of the buds. When buds begin to open the irrigation is reduced until the next flash of buds appear.

Jasminum auriculatum

Local names: Sans.—Juthika, Suchimallika; Hindi—Juhi, Jui; Beng.—Jui; Tel.—Adavimella; Tam.—Usimalligai; Kan.—Vasantamulle; Oriya—Bonsmallika, Jui

The plant is grown in gardens throughout India for its fascinating scented flowers. It is propagated by cuttings. The branches with etiolated base strike easily. Such materials can be obtained by mounding the base of the bush with extra soil for several months.

The plant grows like a shrub but can climb well on support. In home gardens it is usually treated as a climber. In the case of commercial planting it is grown as a dwarf shrub, which facilitates picking of flowers.

Jasminum aungustifolium

Local names: Sans.—Vanamalli; Hindi—Banamallika; Tel.—Chirumalli; Tam.—Kathmallai; Kan.—Vanamallige

The plant is propagated easily by seeds or cuttings. It can be grown in any soil or situation. For its brightly shining deep green foliage and delightfully fragrant flowers *J. aungustifolium* is grown near verandahs or windows with a great interest. It is also trained over a trellis or arbour.

Lawsonia inermis

Local names: Sans.—Mendika; Arabic—Henna; Hindi—Mehendi; Beng.—Mehedi, Mendi; Mar.—Mendhi; Guj.—Medi, Mendi; Tel.—Goranti; Tam.—Marithondi; Kan.—Mayilanchi; Mal.—Mailanchi; Oriya—Benjati; Kashmiri—Mohuz; Punjabi—Mehndi; Mundari—Mindi, Bind

The plant is prized for both its leaves and fragrant flowers. The leaves yield a commercial dye which is used in cosmetics. The large scale cultivation is however mainly as a dye crop and hardly for essential oil. As a commercial dye crop it is cultivated mainly in Punjab and to a small extent in Madhya Pradesh and Rajasthan. The more important centres of production are Faridabad in Punjab and Bardoli and Madhi in Gujarat. The production of *henna* leaves in these centres accounts for 85% of the total production.

Henna is a popular hedge plant and for this reason it is grown widely in Indian gardens. Its thickly branched stems are well adapted for this purpose. Its fragrance is so intense that it sweetens the air all around in rainy months and early winter.

Although it produces large quantities of seed its propagation is mainly done by cuttings. Thick cuttings of two-year-old plants root well during the rains. It can also be propagated by seed during summer or rains. In an experiment seeds were collected in July from a bush and sown immediately. Numerous minute seedlings came up within a week, that grew to a height of 30 cm by the end of September. So it is not necessary to soak the seeds in water for 20-25 days (before sowing) as suggested by some workers.

Although *henna* plants grow in any type of soil, the preference is however given to heavy soil. It can stand a little alkalinity, i.e., pH 9. The plants, rooted cuttings or seedlings, once established continue to grow nicely for 50 years or more even in the harshness of losing leaves successively as a commercial crop. The crop is harvested twice a year April/ May and October/November. For this purpose the bush is cut back to ground, dried up in shade and leaves are separated by beating (Brochure—Marketing Henna, 1955).

In gardens *henna* serves double purpose. The planting along the boundary makes a good hedge and bears fragrant flowers.

Murraya paniculata

Local names: Hindi—Kamini, Marchula; Beng.—Kamini; Mar.—Pandari, Kunti; Tel.—Nagagolungo; Tam.—Ronji; Kan.—Angarakana, Gida; Oriya—Banamallika, Karkankali

It is a member of the illustrious citrus family. Hence its close resemblance to lime or orange in many aspects including flower and fragrance. The plant is very common and popular for its beautiful glossy foliage, thick branching and large clusters of fragrant flowers. It is also a nice hedge plant.

For its small leaves and compact head it is considered a good material for topiary works. Flower buds open in the evening and flowering continues from February-October in several flashes.

Propagation of murraya is simple. Seeds germinate well in summer. Vegetative propagation by cutting or layering is widely followed. Plants grow well in an average soil. There is another species *Murraya elongata* which has larger flower and foliage. Presumably it is due to higher ploidy in its chromosomal status.

In certain areas the plant is subjected to the attack of the citrus-stem borer, *Chalidonium cinctum*. The affected plant may be treated with chloroform and creosote mixture as a remedy.

Nerium (*Nerium indicum*)

Local names: Hindi—Kanch, Karbu, Kuruvira; Beng.—Karavi; Mar.—Kancri; Guj.—Kagaer; Tel.—Ganneru; Tam.—Arali; Kan.—Kanegalu; Mal.—Areli; Oriya—Kancro, Korobiro; Mundari—Kanailiba; Santal—Rajbaka

Nerium is a beautiful flowering shrub for home gardens and parks. The shrub itself is very symmetrical and ornamental. The tips of the slender cane-like stems always bear green foliage. It flowers from February-October. A new cultivar, the yellow Oleander is really a good novelty. The single varieties of nerium bloom profusely and seldom need any care.

Oleander is propagated by cutting or layering. The plant can also be raised from seed. The single varieties are found to set seed in plenty during winter. The viability of seeds is very short. The propagation by seed is not taken up unless longed for any variation. The flexible slender stems are specially suitable for ground layering. A tongue layer roots better than a simple layer. 7-10 cm cuttings taken in winter root in a greater percentage within 60 days. Some growers prefer to put the cuttings in bundles. 10-15 cuttings are made into a bundle and inserted upto 3-4 cm in the rooting medium as usual. For cuttings the use of root hormone and sand medium is recommended. The rooted cuttings or layers should be potted in 20 cm pots with good soil and compost. The transplantation in ground is best suited during the rains.

In an average soil no manuring is in practice. In case the growth is not satisfactory nitrogenous manure and fertilizer should be applied. Where the vegetative growth is heavy at the cost of flowering phosphate and potash should be applied. June-August being a suitable period for manuring.

Pruning is not generally adopted. Only the old thick stems should be pruned to the base to force a number of new basal shoots. For its beautiful shruby growth and showy flowers Oleanders are grown as garden hedge and living screen. Flowering takes place on current year's growth. For good flowering the shoots should have ripened well before setting buds.

The plant is very toxic and poisonous. Because of this property it bears the Sanskrit name 'Asvamarka' which means 'horse killer'. The goat is reported to be able to feed on its foliage though this has been denied by several writers. It proves fatal to camels and all other animals. Several cases of suicide, homicide and abortion by nerium are on record in India. Even honey from its flower is feared to be toxic. Because of the poisonous substances in the plant planting along the boundary does not run the risk of browsing.

Pandanus odoratissimus

Local names: Sans.—Ketaki; Beng.—Keya, Ketaki; Hindi—Keora, Kewda, Ketki, Gagandhul; Mar.—Keora; Guj.—Kewoda; Tel.—Mugali, Gajanzi; Tam.—Tazhari, Thalay; Kan.—Talemara, Kyad-agegida; Mal.—Kaida, Thala

The plant can be propagated by offsets or suckers. It is very prone to develop adventitious roots. So its propagation is simple. But planting in a dry soil during the dry months must be avoided. It should be borne in mind that the plant is extremely moisture-loving and thrives near the water. It takes 3-4 years to flower after planting.

Though the plants grow in abundance in the coastal region the production of flowers is very limited. In some areas, however, the yield is better. In coastal Midnapur the yield is hardly satisfactory. But in the laterite soil of West Midnapur the plant bears more flowers; perhaps due to the fertile and well-drained soil condition.

Plants grow in great plenty near the water of rivers, canals, fields, marshes, lagoons, ponds, lakes etc. Like palms (date, cocoanut or palmyra) pandanus is a good soil-binder; as such checks erosion effectively. Many farms and fisheries in large plots are protected with its impenetrable spinous vegetative growth alongside the ditch dug at the boundaries.

A well-grown bush of 5-10 years in a fertile and well-drained soil produces 10-40 male spadix per year. Generally no manuring is done in case of pandanus. But it responds well to the use of fertilizers. Any manure mixture containing more phosphate and potash helps produce more flowers.

Large leafspots caused by *Melanconium pandani* may develop from leaf margin inward resulting in the premature defoliation and poor flower production.

Control: Prune off infected leaves and spray the plant with any copper fungicide.

Rose

Local names: Hindi—Gulab; Beng.—Golap

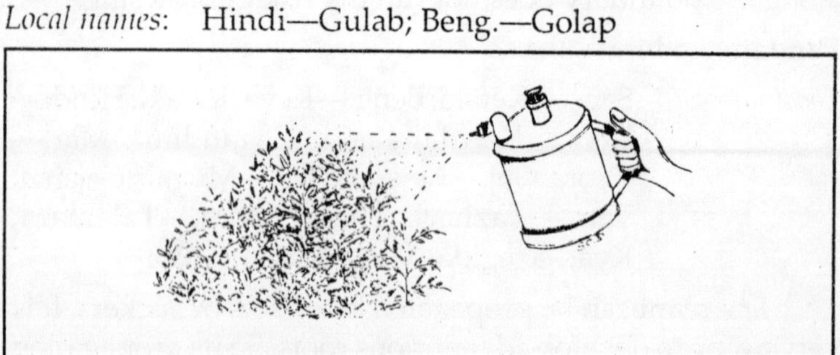

PLANTS BEING SPRAYED WITH PESTICIDES

The hybrid roses have been developed horticulturally by cross-breeding process. They are our modern garden roses. They all are grown for the beautiful and mostly fragrant flowers in a wide range of colours and shades.

The original tea rose is noted for its tea scent. Both tea and damask scent have been derived either freely or blended in the modern roses as a result of complex hybridization using various materials in course of a century. The typical hybrid tea scent is sweet but a bit pungent. The damask scent is very sweet and pleasing. The blends lie in-between. The more the damask predominates the more pleasing will be the perfume.

The rose breeders always aim at infusing sweet perfume among other qualities in the hybrids. Almost all roses have their fragrance. But the number of extremely fragrant roses can be counted on the finger tips. For example, 'Super star' a hybrid tea rose is strongly scented with typical hybrid tea perfume. On the other hand, the reminiscent of strong damask scent can be inhaled from the hybrid tea varieties — 'Sweet Surrender', 'Double Delight', 'Jadis', 'Chrysler Imperial', 'Papa Meilland', 'Mirandy', 'Martin Luther King', 'Oklahoma', 'Etoile de France', 'E.G. Hill', etc. The following is a list of strongly fragrant roses suitable for gardens or cut-flower trade: 'President Poincare', 'Etoile de France', 'Chrysler Imperial', 'Papa Meilland', 'Mirandy', 'Double Delight', 'Avon', 'Oklahoma', 'Super star', etc.

Cultivation: The modern garden roses are mostly delicate. Their root system is not strong enough to grow vigorously. Hence their propagation by grafting onto wild rootstocks. Rose grafts can be grown in ground or pots. Usually a pit 60 cm deep and 40 cm wide is dug just after the rains. The soil of the pit is prepared with plenty of farmyard manure which should be equal to 1/3 of its volume. Super phosphate (100 g) and sulphate of potash (100 g) should be mixed thoroughly with the soil. The pit then prepared is left in a moist condition for a week or so. Then the graft is planted and watered as usual. The average Indian soil is deficient in nitrogen. Secondly it is leached out quickly from the soil. Hence care should be taken to supplement the nutrient from time to time with the application of nitrogenous manures and fertilizers. Oil cake (mustard, *neem* or groundnut), urea, ammonium sulphate, calcium ammonium nitrate are rich in nitrogen which can be used to remove nitrogen deficiency.

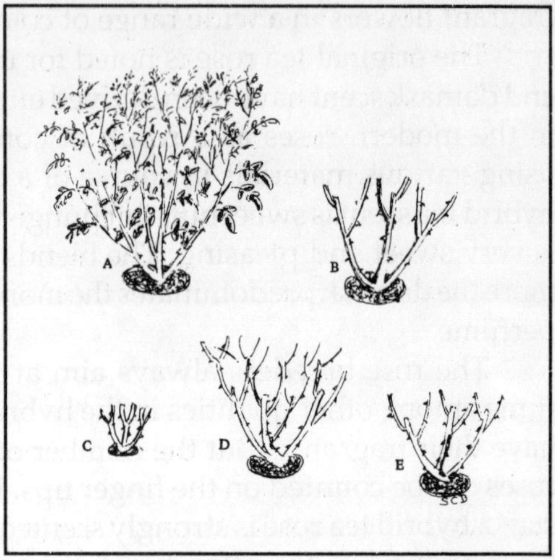

ROSE PRUNING
A. Before Pruning B. After Pruning
C. Hard Pruning D. Light Pruning
E. Medium Pruning

Pruning: The rose, like deciduous plants, tends to remain dormant before the growing season which commences in November in our sub-tropical region. Pruning which consists of the removal of some wood is essential just before the growing season. The removal of dead, diseased, weak and unproductive woods helps restore vigour of the bush.

Removal of the dead, diseased woods should be done as noticed any time of the year for which you need not wait until the annual pruning time comes. You must have a sharp knife or secateurs for a clean cut. Bruising at the cut end may result in the loss of the stem.

Firstly remove all the dead, diseased and weak stems or any portion of stem which has not produced good branches during the last growing season. Then the crossed stems or branches to make an open centre, i.e., the centre of the bush should be in a position to have more light. In this respect one should be careful for the very first pruning to train the bush in a manner that helps spread the stems to all directions leaving the centre free and open. For this purpose a cut should always be made just above a bud pointing outwards or sidewards. In the case of a horizontal branch it may be upwards. A cut is made just 6 to 10 mm above the bud and parallel to the same. If so done, the thinner portion of the cut end will point upwards.

To indicate the height of the stems to be retained after pruning the terms 'hard', 'light' and 'medium' are used. In hard pruning 15-20 cm stems are left from the ground, in light pruning 3/4 of the height of the plant is retained and in medium pruning half of the height of the bush is removed.

i) Hard pruning: It definitely weakens the bush. So one should be judicious if it is imperative. Hard pruning induces strong sprouting from the basal parts. Repeated hard pruning is not recommended. It is practised for the plants of a rich soil. Exhibitors prefer hard pruning to have large blooms.

ii) Light pruning: It is not usually done. If one has to prune his plants in the late season light pruning is recommended. It throws a good number of small weak shoots terminated with drooping flowers.

iii) Medium pruning: It gives a result in-between the two—hard and light pruning. The usual practice being a hard pruning followed by a moderate one in the next season. A beginner who has no experience or lacks confidence should be in the safe side, i.e., adopting moderate or light pruning. A moderate pruning takes less time to cover than the hard and more time than the light (see Pruning in 'Soil and Culture').

The garden rose is susceptible to a number of pests and diseases. Amongst them Blackspot, Mildew, Dieback, Thrips, Scale etc. are serious. Regular spraying with fungicides and insecticides protects the plants from their attack.

CLIMBERS

Artabotrys odoratissimus

Local names: Sans.—Harachampaka; Beng.—Kanthali

champa; Mar.—Hirva champa; S. India—Madarmast, Manoranjtam

Artabotrys odoratissimus is noted for its strong fragrance. Although a climber it can be trained to the form of a thick shrub. The plant itself is very beautiful for its dense dark green glossy leaves. It prefers partial shade. So it can be planted where the majority of the plants will not thrive.

The flowers are not at all showy but their fragrance is inconceivable. The presence of a flower is indicated from a distance by its peculiar fruity fragrance. The flowers being green could not be traced in the midst of thick foliage unless they were so strongly fragrant.

The plant is propagated by seed. Seeds germinate well during the rains. Seedlings are found to grow under the shade of the mother plant. A plant produces plenty of seeds in a region of light soil.

The flowering starts in spring and extends to autumn through the rains. Fruits ripen in winter. The seeds should be sown from April to June in shade. The plant is grown in gardens throughout Eastern India.

Clematis (*C. fammula*)

A slender climber with trifoliate leaves. The flowers are star-like, small (2-2.5 cm) and very fragrant. Petals are linear and four in number.

Clematis flowers in the rains. In a light soil it flowers for a long period, i.e., from June to October. It sets seed. In a clay soil the plant is propagated by the division of clumps or ground layering. But in the region of light soils seed propagation may be adopted. Because of its delicate habit it should be grown with care.

Echites caryophyllata

Local names: Beng.—Malatilata

A heavy climber with white, sweetly scented star-shaped flowers in profusion is an object of beauty during the rains. It thrives both in full sun and partial shade. Obviously it requires a support like a trellis, pergola or an arch. Thinning out or pruning of branches is usually practised when the rain is over. The plant is propagated by layering during the rains. Manuring is not usually practised. But at the time of planting the pit should be manured with cow-manure, bonemeal, woodash etc. until the plant becomes sufficiently large. An annual top dressing with fertilizer mixture should be applied at the beginning of the rains.

Quisqualis indica (Syn. *Q. densiflora*)

Local names: Hindi—Rangoon-ki-beli; Guj.—Baramasi veli; Tel.—Ettaguttilativva; Tam.—Irangunmalli; Bombay—Baramasi, Lalchameli

The plant is a hardy creeper grown widely in gardens for its most popular sweet scented flowers. It can be trained as a shrub or a climber over pergolas, trellises or arches. The abundance of beautiful flowers in drooping clusters creates an intense attraction. The flowers open in the evening as white flowers, gradually changing to pink by morning and to deep red by late afternoon. A few varieties have been distinguished in which variations are mainly in flower colour and leaf size.

The plant is propagated easily by cuttings, layers. It suckers profusely sometimes showing a weedy character in the garden. The plant rarely bears fruits in northern and eastern India.

Quisqualis requires pruning every year for fresh shoots. The thin old shoots from the long canes should be pruned. The long thick canes seldom require shortening unless necessitated for keeping the growths within bounds.

Passion Flower (*Passiflora caerulea*)

Local name: Jhumkolata

It is a heavy climber with abundance of dark-green foliage. Flowers are very beautiful, attractive and deliciously fragrant. It flowers during summer and the rains when the profusion of lush-green foliage masks the solitary blooms of predominantly bluish mauve colour.

The plant is propagated easily by cuttings taken preferably in spring. In light soil it sends out suckers to a long distance, which can be readily used for propagation.

The plant is trained over arches, trellises or pergolas. It makes a good screen when trained along a wire fencing over a compound wall of low height. Pruning is required at an interval of a few years, which should be done when the flowering period is over.

BULBOUS PLANTS

Eucharis grandiflora

Local names: Beng.—Dolan champa

It is a good bulbous plant of sweet-scented flowers. Leaves are large, ovate-lanceolate, about 45 cm long and dark green in colour. It prefers hilly region and moist climate. Flowers come in the rains. 5-7 large white scented flowers are borne in a scape. It responds well in a semi-shade condition. Eucharis grows better in a pot. It, like amaryllis, should be left in a pot for a long time, say, 4-8 years.

Hedychium coronarium

Local names: Beng.—Dulal champa

Hedychium flowers during summer and rains. Delicious fragrant flowers open in the afternoon. As the herb is rhizomatous the propagation can easily be done by division of rhizomes as in the case of canna.

Heavy alluvial loam is suitable for the plant. A dry summer is not favourable for its growth and flowering. During winter the plant does not grow well and all old leaves dry out. The season's growth starts with the rise in day temperature in spring. That time it needs irrigation. In the absence of irrigation water occasional showers in summer due to nor-wester cause sprouting from the rhizome.

Top dressing with cow-manure and fertilizer mixture in summer and regular irrigation cause vigorous growth and heavy flowering.

Lilium

Other name: Easter lily

It is known that liliums were grown in the western part of Asia even 3500 years ago. Amongst its cultivated species 49 are Asian, 24 North American and 2 European.

Although a bulbous plant lilium has a long stem. So most of them need staking. It has many varieties which bear very beautiful and fragrant flowers.

The petals of many varieties are marked with dots of a different colour. The petals (5-6) are beautifully curved backward. The margins of the petals, like glory lily, are wavy. A species named '*L. aurantium*' created a furore in the show of the National Horticultural Society (England) in 1862. Its white petals had yellow stripes and purple dots. It had also perfume like other cultivars.

Lilium has many species and numerous varieties. It is propagated by bulbs.

Orchid

Epiphytic orchids have a special type of roots with a porous corky substance called 'velamen' capable of absorbing and retaining moisture for a long time. Such orchids are found to grow on the tree trunks mostly in the rain forest. On this account the potting procedure should be adapted so as to provide good aeration as enjoyed in their natural environments. Perforated shallow pots (pan shaped) or baskets are selected for potting orchids. The compost comprises fibrous or porous materials. The quick rotting materials are harmful to roots. The suitable materials are osmunda fern roots, polypodium fern roots, tree fern blocks, bark etc. The materials should be clean, i.e., dirt free. They are chopped into pieces. The potting compost also includes some pieces of brickbats (overburnt), charcoal and bone. The use of brickbats and charcoal is for good drainage and that of bone pieces for supplying the phosphatic nutrient.

One third of the pot is filled with small pieces of broken bricks. Then hold the plant with left hand just at the level of the rim and roots inside the pot. Put the wads of the compost round the roots and make it tight with a small planting stick. Be sure it is sufficiently firm. Until the compost does not get decomposed or the same becomes acid it does not need repotting. Generally at an interval of 2-3 years the compost is changed. The operation is known as 'repotting'. It should be borne in mind that the orchids do not like decayed compost and frequent disturbances. Complete stripping down of compost should be avoided. The major part, however, can be replaced with the fresh compost.

Orchids grow well in the diffused sun. The direct morning sun is however helpful. The delicate orchid cannot stand the direct sun. Only short exposures after daybreak and before sundown prove useful. In nature they grow on the branches of the trees of the rain forest. In order to provide the right environment they should be reared in greenhouses, conservatories or under a shade of wooden laths, bamboo splits or green creepers. For orchids a greenhouse is absolutely necessary in cold countries, because artificial heating is needed when the temperature goes below 25°F. In the places of heavier rainfall a glass or alkathene shed is also necessary, because delicate orchids prefer high humidity but not frequent showers.

Watering:

i) Rain water is preferable to tap water. For certain orchids rain water is exclusively used.

ii) Alkaline, saline or cold water should not be used.

iii) Water copiously when watering. An everyday practice of religious sprinkling is not recommended.

iv) Overwatering and water-logging are both detrimental to the health of orchids.

v) Use a water can with its fine rose which helps control the amount of water to be given.

vi) Orchids of hanging pots or baskets need more water because these containers run dry quickly.

vii) Some species become dormant before flowering.

In their dormancy they need not be watered. Mist or fog in morning hours are sufficient to maintain necessary humidity about the roots for the rest of the day. Of course this is the condition that prevails in their natural environments.

In the garden condition, however, one should do the needful to provide such condition.

Damping:

i) Orchids are very fond of atmospheric humidity. Their roots can absorb moisture from the humid air. Hence damping of the surroundings is an important operation of orchid culture.

ii) Spraying the floor, walls and benches with water increases the humidity of the orchid house.

iii) By using sprinklers at a certain interval the required amount of humidity can easily be maintained.

Fragrant Varieties: See 'Cut-flower Trade'.

Tuberose (*Polyanthes tuberosa*)

Local names: Hindi—Gulcheri, Gulshabbo; Beng.—Rajanigandha; Tel.—Sukandaraj, Nelasampengi; Tam.—Nilasam, Pangi; Kan.—Sugandharaj

Its generic name *Polianthes* comes from *polis* a city and *anthos* a flower, meaning 'flower of the city' and should not be confused with 'Polyantha', a group of the garden rose. The name 'Flower of the City' implies that the plant is used for city decorations. But some think that the name derives from the Greek *polios*, white or shining and *anthos*, flower.

From a report it is known that Trover, a Spanish physician, imported the first bulbs from Ceylon (now Sri Lanka) in 1594, and from Spain its cultivation spread to the south-eastern part of France where Peirese was the first grower of the flower.

On account of its strong and slightly intoxicating fragrance it is regarded as the symbol of voluptuousness in the

West, and as such one writer opines that a good girl should not breathe odour of the tuberose in a fine evening or she would hardly be able to get rid of the intoxicating influence.

Tuberose is equally popular in both home gardens and commercial fields for its beautiful and sweet-scented flowers that last for several days and emit perfume in the evening.

Tuberose is propagated easily by offsets. It also sets seeds in certain places. Offsets are small bulbs developed in numbers from the main bulb that puts forth the flowering shoot. The clump of bulbs is dug out in October and offsets are separated. They are preserved in a shed over the winter. In early spring they are planted in well-manured beds in rows about 22-30 cm apart, and about 5 cm deep. Watering should follow just to keep the soil moist until leaves come out, after which regular watering as required should be allowed. The application of manure and fertilizer as top dressing is a usual practice for healthy growth and flowering. For growing tuberose oil cake, bonemeal, woodash should be used. Chemical fertilizers like urea, super phosphate, potassium chloride etc. may also be used.

Tuberose makes a good pot plant. It can also be grown successfully in borders, shrubberies, rockeries. One large bulb per pot should be planted. A good response is obtained with good potting compost. The application of liquid manure (decomposed oil cake and D.A.P.) in a very diluted form at a three-week interval keeps the plant quick-growing.

The double-flowered varieties bloom better in early spring and during the rains. They are considered as a good variety for gardens. Though late they have now become a commodity of cut-flower market. It is a common experience that the developed buds of double-flowered types do not tend to open. It is due to the shortage of nitrogen in the later stage of growth. A dose of a nitrogenous fertilizer few days before the opening of the first pair of buds gives a good result.

It should be borne in mind that one bulb produces only one flower spike; so after flowering a number of offsets begin to develop resulting in a number of plants from the decaying bulb. Manuring as well as other cultural operations should be properly attended to so that the offsets grow quickly. In a light (sandy) soil the offsets do not grow properly due to the shortage of nutrients. This is why tuberose flowers less in a sandy soil.

There are three distinct morphological forms of tuberose flowers—single, semi-double and double. They are all equally fragrant. But the double variety sometimes does not seem so. It opens very slowly and mostly fails to bloom properly. For this reason perfume is not given off as in the case of a timely and properly opened flower. Actually semi-double and double flowers emit more perfume as scent arises from the surface of the petals. Hence more petalage means more perfume. There are also some forms having dwarf spikes (flowering shoots) and others with leaves of white streaks.

ANNUAL HERBS

Alyssum

Popular name: Sweet alyssum

A very low plant having a height of 15-20 cm only. The spreading habit makes the plant bushy. Leaves are very small and light green. Bunches of small white flowers cover the plant. A bed of alyssum in flower looks like a white carpet. Alyssum is a sweetly scented flower which can be grown easily within a very short time. Flowers come up in a six-week old plant. In the plains it flowers from October-March. It is useful for growing in beds, borders and hanging baskets.

September to October being the proper time for sowing seeds which germinate within 4-6 days. The seedlings are very thin. If transplantation is delayed it gives flowers in the seed pans. Transplant the seedlings at a distance of 15-20 cm each way.

A new variety of alyssum named 'Minima' has been originated which is only 5 cm high. It has few colours other than white. They are pink, purple and violet.

Carnation

See 'Commercial Culture of Fragrant Flowers'.

Nicotiana (*N. alata*)

Popular name: Flowering tobacco

Nicotiana has a perennial habit, still it is grown as an annual. The plant is very bushy with its thick branching. The star-like fragrant flowers have a number of colours such as pink, white, red, yellow, purple, violet, maroon etc.

Nicotiana is good for borders and beds. It is also grown in pots. Seeds are very fine, which are sown in September-October. The seedlings at their two-leaf stage can be pricked out and transplanted. Flowering takes place after three months of sowing. Nicotiana prefers light shade.

Sweet Pea (*Lathyrus odoratus*)

Sweet pea is a popular winter annual widely grown in gardens all over the country. Its delicate fragrance, wide range of colours and shades and easy culture are liked by many.

It is a winter annual. Seeds are sown *in situ* in September-October in the plains, and in March and April in the hills. In our sub-tropical region seeds germinate readily. But scarification on seed coats is in practice in cold countries for quick germination. Seeds are large, plump and brown in colour. Wrinkled seeded varieties are also there but they are generally of mauve, lavender or lilac varieties.

Usually seeds are sown in two rows of 30 cm apart. A trellis of wire netting or cord netting is erected in the gap between the rows. The height of the trellis should be of 2 metres for the tall varieties. Seeds germinate within a week. Seedlings are thinned out to maintain a gap of 20 cm between the two plants in a row.

The soil preparation for sweet pea should be deep (30-45 cm) with the use of finely sieved, well-rotted, cow-manure, bonemeal or super phosphate and sulphate of potash or woodash. When the seedling will be 15 cm high liquid manure of oil cake can be applied with advantage. The use of nitrogenous fertilizer is restricted until flower buds appear. Because it causes heavy vegetative growth and delays flowering.

For an exhibition type of blooms cordon system of training as adjusted for grape vines is recommended in which the tip of a seedling of 20 cm height is pinched to force laterals. Only four laterals are selected and retained for growth. The side shoots from the main branches should not be allowed as the inflorescence will be of poor quality. For a good keeping quality of flowers balanced fertilizer must be applied. The seed pots are removed at an early stage for a long period of flowering.

Among the diseases of sweet pea anthracnose, mildew, leafspot etc. are common. The regular use of fungicides controls the diseases. Anthracnose spreads from the seeds raised from infected plants. So care should be taken to collect disease-free seeds. It is safe to treat the seeds with a suitable fungicide before sowing.

Sweet Sultan (*Centaurea moschata*)

A tall annual of 80-110 cm high. Leaf margins are serrated. Flowers look like cornflower, but larger. Colours are white, lilac, red, purple, yellow etc. The scented flowers of sweet sultan are useful for making bouquets and vase decoration.

Seedlings are raised easily from seeds in September to November. They are transplanted 30 cm apart; 3-month-old plants bear flowers.

Reseda

Popular name: Mignonette

The name derives from the Latin word *resedo* meaning 'to heal'. The Romans used the plant to remove the irritation of wounds and disperse abscesses and inflammations. Reseda odorata is grown in gardens for its fragrant flowers. Flowers are greenish yellow or white and strongly perfumed. There are several varieties of this species, the most popular being

'Macbeth' which is compact and strong growing. Its flowers are reddish and commonly grown in pots. The pot-grown plants with flowers are extensively sold in the London markets.

The plants are raised from seeds in September-October. It is very suitable for pot growing. Reseda flowers within three months of sowing seeds. The flowers are small and produced in loose spikes and sweetly scented.

Seeds are sown at permanent sites in pots or beds. After sowing press the seeds on the compost, which facilitates quick germination. The seedlings are thinned out to 15-22 cm apart. Reseda grows best in a light soil. Although moisture loving it should be grown in a well-drained soil in a sunny situation.

COMMERCIAL CULTURE OF FRAGRANT FLOWERS FOR CUT-FLOWER TRADE

Tuberose (*Polyanthes tuberosa*)

Amongst the fragrant flowers tuberose and jasmine occupy a very prominent place in the fresh flower trade. Delightfully fragrant flowers of tuberose remain fresh for a pretty long time. Moreover it stands transit to distant markets in a simple packing. The vase life of a tuberose spike is also longer which varies from 8-15 days depending upon the care taken and the temperature and humidity of the surrounding. Hence its extensive popularity.

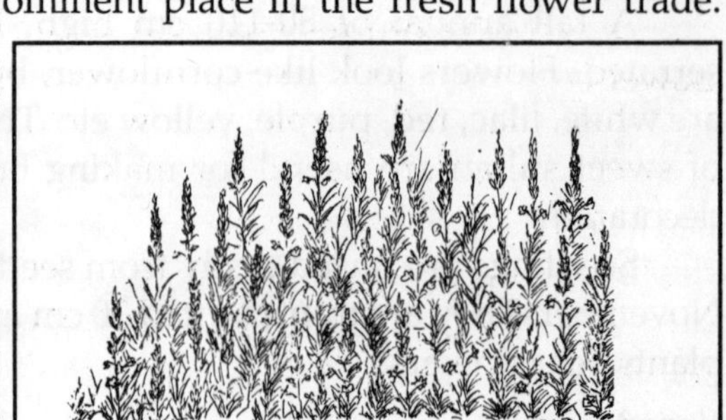

FIELD OF TUBEROSE

For the purpose of commercial cultivation care should be taken to raise standard-size tubers in good quantities which serve as the planting material for a good crop of flower in a short span. In view of this small offsets are graded and planted separately 5-10 cm apart in a bed. To lessen the cost of production through saving expenses the offsets are set out on the eve of the monsoon and lifted in November. Weeding, hoeing are common cultural operations which should not be neglected in course of cultivation. Another source of having large bulbs is the clumps exhausted after flowering. 8-10 large sized bulbs can be obtained per clump at the end of the third year's growth.

Tuberose is widely cultivated in Italy, Holland, United States and Cape of Good Hope for its bulbs which are exported to other countries. The bulbs imported from outside flower better in Great Britain than those grown indigenously. The commercial production of tuberose bulbs can itself be a different industry that can grow in the interior of the country lying far off from the flower growing centres near the major cities (Dey, S.C.—Commercial Production of Tuberose Bulbs, 1980).

About 1200-1500 kg bulbs are required to plant one hectare of tuberose. The supply of standard bulbs to the flower growing centres enables the growers to raise their flower crop within a few weeks. This will also attract more new growers who can take up flower growing as an interim crop in a short gap. For such a short-term crop the planting can be timed to harvest on the special festive dates on which the price touches the peak. The first grade bulbs (30-35 mm diam) planted on the 10th day of March may yield flowers on the 20th May, i.e., after 70 days of planting in the plains.

For its culture in the conventional method the soil should be prepared by ploughing thoroughly for a good tilth. Use manure and fertilizers as given below for an acre of planting. Bidhan Chandra Krishi Viswavidyalaya (Kalyani, Nadia, West Bengal) has recommended NPK 2:3:2 for growing tuberose.

Farmyard manure/compost	5 m^3
Oil cake (pulverised)	300 kg

Super phosphate (single)	110 kg
Muriate of Potash	72 kg
Urea	60 kg

Apply the above mixture by broadcasting. Care should be taken to mix it into the tilth. The total quantities of oil cake and urea, however, should be applied in three equal split doses: once during the preparation of soil, the second, two months after planting and the third should be applied one month after the second dose. Leave the field in a moist condition for 2-3 weeks, after which the planting of bulbs should be done. The bulbs are planted 60 cm deep in beds from February-May in the plains and April-June in the hills. The shallow planting encourages more side growths as offsets. The bulbs in rows are set 30 cm apart. The distance between the two adjacent rows is also 30 cm. A spacing of 60 cm is kept between the fourth and fifth rows. When the standard bulbs are planted for only a 8-12 week crop they are planted very closely: 40 bulbs are set per square metre.

In the places of low temperature in winter the bulbs remain dormant for a long period. If an early planting is required the bulbs should be treated with 4% theourea solution (dip the bulbs in the solution for an hour). Another way is to soak the bulbs in warm water for a few hours and then place them inside a compost heap. After a week or so the bulbs can be planted when sprouting starts.

In winter bulbs remain perfectly dormant if preserved in a dry and dark place. In the places of mild winter bulbs stored in the lighted place show their slow growth. Even tiny offsets are found to grow and they become green in colour. While planting such tiny offsets should be rubbed off, or flowering will be delayed. Irrigate the crop when the bulbs have started their growth. Weeding, hoeing and other cultural operations should be done regularly.

In the plains of India where winter is mild tuberose flowers throughout the year; although in lesser quantities from November-January. Consequently the price becomes very high during this period of lean production. The expert growers are found to force the plants with plenty of nitrogenous fertilizer. During the end of October they apply manures and fertilizers after hoeing and weeding for this purpose. A mixture of compost, pulverised oil cake, hoof and hornmeal and *suphala* (15:15:15) is generally used.

In West Bengal the flower growing area near Kolaghat in the district of Midnapore has traditionally been growing tuberose for the Calcutta market. Recently a new area near Ranaghat in the district of Nadia has taken up tuberose growing with a higher rate of production. Nearly 1200 hectares of the adjacent area have already been brought under tuberose cultivation. Tuberose prefers clay soil. The soil of Kolaghat area is heavy and that of Ranaghat is slightly loose textured and granular. Hence highly suitable for tuberose culture. The soil fertility of both areas is high; still the agro-technique is different. The growers of Nadia, however, rely more on the use of chemical fertilizers, and as such the rate of production is higher. But the flowers do not last longer. On the contrary, the flowers raised in the Kolaghat area where organic manures like compost, oil cake and hoof and hornmeal are the main ingredients for enriching the tuberose fields, fetch a better price for their long life. In both the areas a crop once raised flowers for three years. During the third year of growth declining is apparent.

Flowering starts after 60 days of planting. The first spikes came from the bulbs which were planted originally and the next flashes are from the offsets that grow round the main bulbs. Gradually, offsets increase in number forming a clump. The flowering shoots come up more and more until the end of the second year, after which the rate of production decreases owing to the rise of numerous offsets. For this reason one crop is retained for three years and then it is removed. The production reaches its peak during the second year. At the end of third season irrigation is stopped in order to make the bulbs ready for digging out. A few days before lifting the leaves are cut down from the ground level with a garden sword. The digging operation itself is same as with the tubers of potato. Each clump produces 20-35 bulbs of which 10-15 have attained a good size. These are considered a by-product. The surplus bulbs are disposed of to new growers. A good sum can be obtained out of it if exported to other countries.

The bulbs should be graded according to their size. Loose scales and long roots should be removed. For a first few days they are stored in an open place so that excess moisture runs dry. Then keep them in a dark, dry and well-ventilated room until planted in the season. It is better to keep them in bamboo baskets than to pack them in paper-board cartons.

The commercial cultivation of tuberose demands a rich heavy soil. In a light sandy soil deficiency of nutrients occurs rapidly. Hence the tuberose growing may not be profitable. But the improved technique of culture removes the difficulty, which recommends to hold the crop for a season only; and fertilize in short intervals in split doses. The bulbs should be planted deeply so that offsets grow less. In a light soil the bulbs tend to develop more offsets in a very short time, which severely compete for nourishment. For this reason, only a limited number of offsets should be allowed to grow.

In a rich soil the traditional practice is to hold the crop for three years. The farmers prefer this method as it helps obtain three winter crops which fetch a good price due to a heavy demand for the lean production. In a region of mild winter tuberose continues to bloom all through winter months provided the crop is properly attended to with manuring and irrigation. Still the grower should be aware of the modern technique developed through experiments in small plots. In a plot of 4 m^2 196 standard bulbs (30 mm diam) weighing 20 grams each were planted in clay soil (heavy loam) near Kolaghat on 17th February 1981. The bulbs were planted 15 cm apart each way. Farmyard manure (50 l), pulverised mustard cake (5 kg), super phosphate (500 g) and muriate of potash (400 g) were mixed up to the tilth of 20 cm three weeks before planting. The soil was kept moist for the period from manuring to the sprouting of leaves from the planted bulbs. Afterwards irrigation was given as required. The field of tuberose of the vicinity needed only five irrigations from the middle of February to the end of May. Few interim showers saved irrigation. The flowering shoots began to appear from the 21st March and the flowers were picked from 9th April of the same year. The flowering shoots from the bulbs planted were over before the 15th May. Then the offsets began to develop from the spent up bulbs. A gap of flowering for around four weeks was noticed after which flowers were harvested regularly until the end of January. The total number of spikes obtained from April to January was 588 that produced flowers weighing nearly 6 kg.

The special technique adopted was to allow only 3 offsets to grow from each bulb. For quick fattening of those offsets liquid manure were applied at a fortnight interval from April to December.

The rate of production of this type of intensive culture is very high and hence encouraging, especially to those who hold a small plot of land.

Diseases and Pests: Tuberose growing is not usually troubled by pests and diseases. However, leaf rotting has been reported which is caused by a fungus—*Sclerotium rolfsii* (Das, Science and Culture, 1961). The remedial measure lies in the application of fungicides. This disease is however very serious, which hardly occurs in areas with clay soil. The incidence of the disease should not be neglected.

The commercial importance of different varieties: On the basis of the flower-form three varieties are found in this country. But to evaluate the performance the cultivars from the different parts of the country were collected and grown in Coimbatore under the Faculty of Horticulture of the Tamil Nadu Agricultural University. Amongst them four single (Bombay Single, Calcutta Single, Coimbatore Single, Single Mexican), one semi-double (from Calcutta) and five double types (Calcutta Double, Double Pearl, Pant Nagar, Bangalore and Coimbatore) were tried.

Amongst the singles 'Calcutta Single' and 'Mexican Single' gave better yield of flowers. The double-flowered cultivar 'Pearl' performed better than other two double types.

The semi-double variety has no stability. It often changes to single form. So it cannot be regarded as a variety.

Rose

Both for fresh-flower market and essential-oil industry the demand of rose knows no bounds. But the commodity is different for the said purposes. For example, modern garden roses are used as cut flowers while for oil extraction the old damask rose is mainly grown.

In five big cities of India Bombay, Calcutta, Madras, Delhi and Bangalore 705 tons of rose blooms are sold daily, but they are mainly for garlands, bouquets, wreaths etc. In the developed countries the demand is much higher. Not only that, the quality of flowers they demand is much superior to those which are sold in India.

Amongst the tea roses 'Gruss-an-Tepliz' (also known as Kalkattia) and 'Etoile de France' dominate our cut-flower markets. Though sweet scented they lack other essential qualities like good shape, attractive colour, long vase life etc. Recently, however, other hybrid teas of good shape and colour are in demand in our inland market. The florist shops in the sophisticated market display such roses with long stems in their show-cases. Amongst them 'Montezuma', 'Madam Curie', 'Lal Bahadur', 'picture', 'super star' etc. are preferred to others.

The region from Kolaghat to Kharagpur in the district of Midnapore is noted for growing roses for the cut-flower market of Calcutta. The rich clay soil irrigated with tank water yields a good harvest of roses resulting in low market price which ranges from Rs. 4-12 per bunch of hundred flowers. This is perhaps the cheapest market of cut-flowers in India. Since the pre-independence period the region near Madhupur and Deoghar of Bihar has been supplying cut-roses to the Calcutta market in winter. Nowadays this supply has decreased to the minimum on account of the heavy local supply. In those days the demand of roses among the Britishers in Calcutta led to the creation of a rose-growing centre in Madhupur and Deoghar where roses grow well in the laterite soil.

Once the Viceroy of India was celebrating the X-mas festival in the Belvedere Palace of Alipur (Calcutta). A large quantity of red roses was due to arrive from Madhupur to Calcutta by train on that occasion. The floral consignments were booked at the railway station for transporting to Calcutta through the Punjab Mail. Due to the short stoppage of the Punjab Mail at Madhupur station the consignment could not be entrained. So the train left the station without the flowers. Immediately the information was sent to the Viceroy who ordered the railway authority to send back the Punjab Mail from its present position to Madhupur to carry the packings containing flowers. It is very interesting to notc the order was carried out immediately.

For cut-flowers roses are grown outdoors or indoors. The former being the normal ground culture and the latter, greenhouse culture.

Here we will dwell on normal culture in the ground.

The selected varieties having the qualities of a cut-flower will be grafted on to the hardy rootstock of *Rosa multiflora*. The following varieties are suitable for cut-flowers in our inland market: Gruss-an-Tepliz, Etoile de France, super star, Madam Curie, Queen Elizabeth, etc.

The planting distance depends on the fertility of the soil—in an area of rich soil the distance between plant to plant being from 1-1.5 m. For soil preparation, planting and feeding the methods recommended for *Rosa damascena* can be followed. As regards pruning, other cultural operations and protection against pests and diseases the methods as laid down for hybrid tea roses (in Chapter 2) should be adopted

Jasminum sambac

The buds of sambac are in great demand in fresh flower market in India. For its floriferous habit and strongly scented flowers sambac is a popular item in home gardens as well as commercial culture. For cut flowers extremely floriferous varieties are selected. The plot of land must be sunny and have a gentle slope to one side for good drainage of surplus water. The plant is propagated by one-year-old stem cuttings. Make holes 15 cm deep and 50 cm apart in a row. The distance between the two adjacent rows is 150 cm. 5-8 cuttings of 30 cm long should be planted in a hole just on the eve of monsoon. The cuttings will take nearly four weeks to strike. The root eruption will correspond to the emergence of new leaves. Protect the tender leaves against the insect attack by insecticides (Metacid 50/Metacystocks). Take care of the plants by paying attention to all necessary cultural operations. In a year the plants attain a good height. Apply top dressing with the following mixture in the first week of February. After weeding fork the soil of the rows and apply manure. The mixture of the following ingredients is for a ten-metre space of the row:

Cow-manure	60 litres
Oil cake (pulverised)	2 kg
Hoof and hornmeal	1 kg
Super phosphate	500 g
Muriate of potash/woodash	500 g

Generally two irrigations are required in a month in a clay-soil area. Just before an irrigation apply urea (100g/sq m) by broadcasting once in a month. During the first year the vegetative growth should be encouraged and as such all flower buds should be removed at their early stage. From the second year flower buds are secured and picked for the market. The peak period starts from the third year which may last for 15 years or more.

J. sambac blooms over a long period from March to October. In order to force early flowering to meet the demand the market growers prune the bushes at the height of 60 cm in late winter and apply manure and fertilizer liberally. The forcing must be preceded by a dry condition in the field to make the bushes dormant. It becomes perfect for heavy blossoms if the plants are denuded of leaves or the leaves retained are stripped off at the time of pruning. The frequency of irrigation is determined by the growth of shoots and flower buds. Until flower buds appear irrigation should be normal; and then increased to provide more moisture for rapid growth of the buds. When first picking is started irrigation is stopped until the next flash of buds appears.

In *J. sambac* six varieties were evaluated. The cv 'Gundumall' recorded the highest flower yield of 8.12 tons which was closely followed by the cv 'Iruvatchi' with 6.93 tons of flowers per hectare.

The measures against pests and diseases are same as given in case of *J. auriculatum.*

Jasminum auriculatum

Although *auriculatum* is grown as a climber in home gardens the market growers for the convenience of picking flowers grow it as a very bushy shrub. For a large-scale propagation the use of cuttings is best. The stem cuttings (green or brown) of 20 cm long taken in the rains strike well. Small plants are transplanted 2 m apart each way in the field. The bushes give flowers from the third year of planting. In February pruning is necessary which must be followed by manuring as well as irrigation. Flowering starts in April and continues to the end of August. The cultural operations are almost same as given for *J. grandiflorum* in 'Field Culture of Fragrant Flowers for Perfumery Industry'.

In *Jasminum auriculatum* there are five varieties of which the cv 'Short Round' recorded the highest flower yield, followed by 'Long Round' (Syn. Co1, Mullai).

J. auriculatum is reported to be affected by shooty mould caused by *Meliola jasminocola* P Henn, which can be controlled by spraying wettable sulphur.

Carnation (*Dianthus caryophyllus*)

The carnation is a very popular garden plant treated as an annual or perennial. It is broadly classified into three groups — Border, perpetual-flowering and Marguerite or Chabaud. The modern breeding and selection have given rise to many other types. Amongst the various types the perpetual-flowering is by far the best. It was first sold for a fantastic price of 30,000 dollars, thereby creating a sensation all over the world and winning the worldwide popularity. On account of better keeping quality the perpetual-flowering types have secured a good place in the cut-flower trade.

In this country carnations are grown in gardens as annuals. Only in the hills they are preserved as a perennial. When grown as an annual they are raised from seed. Propagation by cuttings or layers is adopted in case of old stocks preserved as dahlias or chrysanthemums. Carnation grows to a height of 45-75 cm. The popularity of carnation lies mainly in its strong clove-like fragrance, excellent form of flowers with lasting quality and wide range of colours — clear white, yellow, red, scarlet, violet, dark crimson and many intermediate shades. An ideal soil for carnation is sandy loam.

Seeds are sown early as the plant takes a long period of growth before flowering. The flowering period being from February to May. Seeds are sown in August-October in the plains. Seedlings come up within a week. After a month they become ready for transplantation. Carnation, like chrysanthemums, is a lime-loving plant. So a soil with acidic reactions must be avoided. Organic manures like cow-manure, compost or leafmould should be worked into the soil during its preparation. Because organic manures in contact with the stems may cause stem rot. The use of nitrogenous fertilizers during the later stage of growth should be restricted as it tends to produce a lush vegetative growth which yields poor-quality blooms.

Carnation needs staking to stand upright as it is a scandent herb. Stopping and disbudding are essential practices of carnation culture. The tips of the young plants when 25 cm high are pinched off to force strong basal shoots. They also in their turn are stopped to make the plant more bushy. Each branch is terminated with a number of buds. In order to have the good quality blooms only the central bud should be retained and the small side buds must be pinched out. Some flowers may have a defect of splitting calyx which is usually a hereditary character. This can be prevented by tying string before anthesis.

When flowering is over the stools are pruned leaving 12 cm from the ground. This is done with a view to preserving the plant for the next year. The climates of the hills are quite suitable for this purpose. The stool however is to supply a number of shoots for cutting or layering. Spring or autumn is the suitable time for the vegetative propagation. The cuttings are selected from the side shoots without any flower buds. The cuttings with lower leaves trimmed are treated with root hormone and inserted into a sand medium. They strike within 4-6 weeks. Bottom heat is useful which quickens root eruption. The other method of vegetative propagation is tongue layering which is surer than the former. If root hormone is applied on the cut-side of the tongue early root formation is stimulated.

For raising quality cut flowers feeding should be judiciously done to secure strong growth. Because the soft growth yields soft blooms that lack keeping quality. Sheep manure (decomposed and pulverised), dried blood and potassium sulphate are very useful for this purpose. Disbudding as stated already must be followed for having large blooms.

The seedlings in the seed pan or after transplanting may rot due to damping off. Overcrowding of seedlings, lack of drainage in the pot soil, use of old infected soil etc. aggravate the incidence. To stop the loss of seedlings care should be taken to sow seeds thinly, make the drainage hole clear and use fresh compost every time. Treating seeds and soils with fungicides is also in practice to prevent the disease. After the emergence of seedlings the soil can be drenched with 20% Captan solution and the process can be repeated at a five-day interval, if necessary.

The stem-rot disease which is most prevalent is caused by a fungus — *Pellicularia filamentos*. It causes sudden wilt resulting in the decay of the stems just below the soil surface. To control the trouble drenching the soil with 20% Captan solution is recommended.

Commercial Production: The Punjab Agricultural University (Ludhiana) has been making efforts since 1973 to standardise the agro-technique for the commercial production of carnation. Their recommendations are laid down here. A space of one square metre should accommodate 25 plants thus each occupying 400 c^2. An analysis of 40 g N, 10 g P_2O_5 and 10 g K_2O per m^2 gives maximum yield of quality blooms. An yield of 400-500 flowers can be harvested per m^2, out of which about 20 per cent will be blue grade, 40 per cent red grade and 40 per cent green grade flowers (Aurora and John 1976).

FIELD CULTURE OF FRAGRANT FLOWERS FOR PERFUMERY INDUSTRY

Jasminum grandiflorum

The Grasse region of Southern France has become world famous for the large-scale cultivation of *J. grandiflorum* over 200 years for flower-oil industry. As it was first introduced from Spain *J. grandiflorum* is also known as 'Spanish Jasmine' in France. The extensive cultivation of jasmine in fact has given rise to that unique and charming essential-oil industry.

In France *J. grandiflorum* grown on its own root is found to be susceptible to root disease and frost damage. Hence they are grafted onto *J. officinale* that grows wild on their mountains. The rootstocks are planted very closely allowing only 800 sq cm to each of them. Thus one hectare usually accommodates 100,000-150,000 stocks. There they are grafted *in situ* next year. The bushes are trimmed every year to keep them low so as to facilitate picking of flowers. The production of flowers from such fields varies from 3000-4000 kg per hectare per annum.

It is obvious that manuring, irrigation and weather conditions also play an important role in raising a good crop of flowers. In sunny and warm weathers flowers contain more perfume. In India, however, flowering season is warm to hot but mostly rainy. Hence much of the perfume is likely to be washed down by showers between opening and picking of flowers. Though the buds open in the evening the perfume content becomes highest at daybreak. As the day advances the volatile perfume gradually vaporises and disappears at about 10 A.M. The picking of flowers has to be done carefully, preferably by skilled women or girls. A skilled hand can collect 500 grams of jasmine in an hour.

In France one plantation does not last longer than 10-15 years. The dying out of stocks in increasing numbers demands a new plantation. Italy, Egypt and Morocco are the countries that have developed the industry lately. They grow jasmine in their own way. Because of the mild winter in Sicily and Calabria the damage by frost does not occur, and as such raising stocks by grafting is not followed. The layers or cuttings are grown in the nursery and set out in the field after a year. The average yield recorded is 5000 kg per hectare.

Near Cairo jasmine is being grown since 1912 for oil extraction. The cultivation practices followed are more or less like those of Italy. The layers are planted 1 m apart in a row. The rows are 2 m apart. The plantation with such spacing comprises 5000 shrubs per hectare. The individual shrubs, unlike in France, are allowed to grow much larger.

In Morocco the first attempt to grow jasmine for extraction of its perfume on an industrial scale was made in 1941. In growing jasmine the cultural practices adopted in vineyards of Algeria were followed. Much larger bushes were trained against the trellis as done for grapes. The process of heavy manuring was preferred. Frequent dressings with large quantities of fertilizer and manure, weekly hoeing and irrigation were in the cultural programme during the flowering period. Besides two major cultivations per year were a must. These ensure the prospect of a bumper harvest of more than 6000 kg per hectare of plantation at its peak periods.

In India one firm named Encee Ltd. near Mettupalayam has in the last decade employed *J. grandiflorum* for extraction of its perfume on a modern industrial scale. The information on agro-technique, cultivar etc. has not yet been available. The flower production of *J. grandiflorum* is very satisfactory in the southern states. A cultivar 'Co1' was recorded by the Tamil Nadu Agricultural University in Coimbatore as a very high yielding variety. In Eastern India the yield is irregular and mostly unsatisfactory. In the heavy soil of lower Bengal the vegetative growth tends to be heavy at the cost of flowering. But the laterite zone of Eastern India is more or less suitable for good flowering. In the Indian climate flowering season during the rains saves the irrigation cost. But the loss of perfume by showers is a problem; secondly the field abounds in weeds that share the nutrients of the soil. The leaching out of nitrogenous fertilizers applied during the flowering season with surplus water also increases the cost of growing flowers.

The root-gall disease of *J. grandiflorum* tells upon the production. The use of competent rootstocks is the answer. It is customary to select very vigorous and disease-resistant varieties as rootstocks. The author has tried various types of stocks, amongst them *J. multiflorum* is found very suitable in the eastern region. In the northern parts the jasmine is also cultivated on a large scale for the extraction of perfume in Farrukhabad, Ballia, Jaunpur, Ghazipur, etc. The flower yield is very high in Farrukhabad, which is 750 kg per hectare during the peak periods. The plants are propagated by layers or cuttings and planted out in the field in the beginning of the rains. Once established a plant continues to yield flowers over a long period of thirty years.

During the recent years improved agro-technique applied on the high yielding varieties has recorded much higher yields not only abroad but in India also. In France the maximum yield reported is 4,000 kg per hectare. In south India the yield of Co1 (Pitchi) is recorded 10.14 tons per hectare closely followed by 'Thinonapuram' with 10.05 tons of flowers per hectare. *J. grandiflorum* is a fairly hardy and drought resistant plant. Though they grow in a wide variety of soils, loamy or sandy soils are best. In a clay soil the vegetative parts grow profusely at the cost of flowering. It is propagated easily by cuttings, layers or suckers. In moist weather during the rains aerial roots are found to grow from the nodes of branches. If separated and planted they may grow to individual plants. It can also be raised well by sowing seeds in spring or summer. Seeds germinate well within a week or so. Seed setting is regular in southern India. The propagation by budding is easy, which is adopted to grow plants on stocks free from root disease and frost damage.*

The jasmine responds well to the application of balanced fertilizer with humus. Irrigation during the flowering is essential if there is no rain. As it is a climber it needs the support of trellises, arbours or pergolas. In the fields of France bushes are kept as low shrubs by pruning. Hence no support is required.

Many varieties of *J. grandiflorum* are in cultivation in India. The plants grown from seeds often show variations. The best ones are selected and propagated vegetatively, on account of which innumerable varieties are come across.

Rosa damascena

Local names: Hindi—'Bussorah'; U.P.—'Fasli gulab', 'Barwana'; Beng.—'Basrai golap'

The Damask rose is cultivated on a commercial scale in many parts of the world. Nowadays the Balkan States supply a great portion of the commercial rose oil (Otto of Rose) extracted from the Damask rose. But a special rose flower

*The success achieved by the author is above 90 per cent which is contrary to the result given in "Inter-specific Grafting in Jasminum" — Nambisan and Krishnan, 1980.

industry has been developed in southern France where perfume is extracted from the cabbage rose, *Rosa centifolia*. In India the Damask rose is grown for rose-oil and rose-water in the district of Ghazipur (Ghourabad, Gunda, Fasidi and Asmanicha), Ballia (Sikandarpur), Faizabad, Lucknow, Kanpur (Rewatpur, Binayakpur, Bisayakpur, Banger, Kakadev, Lekinpur and HBTI), Farrukhabad (Kannauj), Aligarh, Etah (Jhinwar) and Udaipur (Nathduara-Khamnore).

Soil and climate: Although it is grown in gardens all over India the Damask rose, like most crops, is a chooser of soil and climate for its commercial cultivation. Well-drained alluvial loam of Uttar Pradesh is found suitable for its culture. Rich sandy soil with a good amount of humus is highly recommended for its commercial cultivation.

Propagation: The Damask rose is easily propagated by stem cuttings. In cooler climates small cuttings (3 to 6 cm) root well. But in our hot climate cuttings of 20-25 cm are suitable. Although cuttings root in all seasons they are generally taken in December-January when plenty of branches are obtained after pruning the bushes. About one-year-old canes are selected for cuttings which give the best result. Garden soil instead of sand should be used as a rooting medium. The cuttings may be treated with root hormone for good rooting. 5-8 cm of the cuttings are inserted in the soil. Any suitable insecticide must be applied at the upper end of the cuttings to prevent insects from getting into the soft pith. To be sure against the attack of white ants which destroy the cuttings Aldrin, D.D.T. or BHC or any other substitute must be applied to the soil before and after inserting the cuttings. Rooting takes place in 3-4 week time, which is indicated by corresponding shoot growth of the cuttings. The new rooted cuttings should not directly be transferred to the field. They are potted in small pots (12 cm) at least for three months before transplanting.

Planting: A sunny situation and the facilities for irrigation in summer are absolutely necessary. The distance between the plants should be 1 m in both directions, and this will accommodate about 10,000 plants in one hectare of land. The pits measuring about 45 cm across and 60 cm deep are dug in September to December. 3-4 kg of well-rotted cow-manure or farmyard manure and 100 g of super phosphate should be applied per pit. The planting is done from October to February. Irrigate the plants as necessitated.

Top dressing: The Damask rose is a gross feeder. It needs much nutrition for good growth and bumper crop of flowers. It needs, like garden roses, manuring after pruning in October-December. A commercial fertilizer mixture with farmyard manure should be applied in an optimum quantity. During the growing season 200 kg of nitrogen is required per hectare. The total nitrogen is applied in three equal split doses. 50 kg of P_2O_5 (available in about 200 kg of single super phosphate) is required to be applied in a crop of one hectare. The potassic fertilizer at the rate of 60 kg per hectare should be applied.

Foliar feed is very useful during the period of vegetative growth. It is applied at fortnightly interval and should not be continued after flowering has started. Many proprietary products are available in the market; amongst them Agromin, Multiplex, Vipul etc. have proved to be useful.

Irrigation: Regular irrigation at weekly intervals is a must for higher yields. It should start just after pruning.

Pruning: It is an important cultural operation for forcing the plants for good growth and flowering. Pruning, however, is not required until the plant has become very strong and bushy. The plants are pruned just before the growing season. As the Damask rose is a summer flowering variety pruning should be done in the middle of winter so that the new sprouts can produce flowers in March/April.

In pruning about 30-50 cm wood from the ground is retained. All dead and weak woods should be removed. Sharp spears or secateurs are used for pruning and the cut end should preferably be treated with a fungicide.

Flowering and yield: Although the Damask rose flowers from March to July the peak period being only about 60 days from the middle of March to the middle of May. The weight of a flower varies from 2-2.5 grams, thus 1 kg of flowers number 450 in average.

A temperature range of 25°C-30°C and 60 per cent relative humidity are ideal for optimum flowering (Chandra et al 1970). The average yield of flowers is estimated at about 5000 kg per hectare.

Pests and diseases: The troubles caused by pests and diseases are same as we experience in the case of garden roses. Fungicides and insecticides should regularly be used to keep down or eradicate the trouble-causing agents.

Rosa centifolia

Eng. Vernac.: Cabbage rose

In the British gardens it is known as 'Cabbage rose'. To the French perfumer it is 'Rose de Mai'. It grows wild in the eastern Caucasus. The wild varieties are single-flowered.

Flowers are full globular and strongly scented. Its varieties are 'Robert le Diable' and 'Tour de Malakoff'. In India it is grown in U.P. and Bihar. The agro-technique to be adopted is more or less same as recommended for the Edward rose. The 'Cabbage rose' has a sport which is known as 'Moss rose'. It is characterized by a sweety scented moss-like growth of hairs with oil glands on the sepals, which emit perfume. It also has few varieties; amongst them 'Celina', 'Nuits de young' and 'Old pink Moss' are popular.

Edward Rose (*Rosa Edouard*)

Varieties: Deshi, Cheenia and Kaithal

Cheenia and Deshi are also called *Baramasi* which means bearing flowers throughout the year. The *Cheenia gulab* of Kanauj has purple flowers with fragrance stronger than that of other cultivars of the Edward rose. The popularity of the cultivars of the Edward rose lies in that they flower for 10 months in N. India and throughout the year in the Southern States. Previously the Edward rose was used as a rootstock for bud grafting. Nowadays it is mostly replaced by R. indica (cv Odorata). The flowers of the E. rose are mainly used for making rose water, rose recipes and hair oils. They are also used in Ayurvedic drugs and cold drinks (*Thandai*). As a cut flower E. rose is used in making garlands and offering to deities in temples.

In south India the E. rose is popularly known as Rajapoo (in Tamil). In a number of places of Tamil Nadu and Karnataka the E. rose is grown for producing rose water. Tanjore being the largest centre of manufacturing rose water in the South.

The agro-technique as recommended for the Damask rose can be followed for the Edward rose. But it should be borne in mind that it needs more manure and fertilizer than any other rose. 200 kg of nitrogen per hectare in three split doses should be applied. A liberal amount of farmyard manure, say 10-12 tons per hectare, should be applied after pruning each season. For the soil preparation for planting the same quantity of manure is required. The phosphate and potash in the form of bonemeal and woodash respectively can be used as usual.

The Edward rose blooms longer than the Damask rose. Besides the proper season (March-April) its flowering occurs for the second and the third times during monsoon (July-August) and autumn (October-November). In winter buds appear but do not open. In Peninsular India winter is not strong; for this reason the E. rose blooms there throughout the year.

The experiments at HBTI, Kanpur have proved that the quality of Otto produced from our roses (Bussorah and Edward) is not inferior to that of Bulgaria.

Kewda (*P. odoratissimus*)

Kewda is an economic plant that has potentiality for earning immense wealth from abroad thereby opening employment potentialities in rural India in essential oil industries. It grows in any soil near water. Its purposeful mass plantation has not yet been undertaken. Apart from the individual endeavours village *Panchayats, Anchal panchayats* and social forestry wing of the Government forest departments can do well for its mass cultivation. The erosion of soils near the water courses, river sides, river mouths, estuaries, sea coasts etc. has become a common problem. Its prolific aerial roots (stilt roots) bind the soil and check erosion effectively which manifests the importance of its cultivation. The vegetative parts of the plant are also in use. The bark of the long stilt roots is extensively used in basketry as a substitute of cane.

As the *kewda* leaves are highly prickly the new plantation does not need any protection from cattle and goats. As it does not yield any timber or firewood the plantation hardly attracts felling like forest or road-side trees. Like other resources the potentialities of *kewda* should be understood, which would then lead to its mass cultivation. *Kewda* plantation, unlike other crops, can be raised on a large scale without tears.

Citrus aurantium

The sour orange is cultivated all over the world for fruit preserves and essential oil. In India, however, it is used mostly in pickles. Essential oil is obtainable both from flowers and peels. Sour orange is grown on a commercial scale near Seville (Spain) for its fruits which are supplied in large quantities to England and Scotland for use in preparing marmalade.

Seeds and seedlings are in great demand in nurseries. The seedlings of sour orange are considered best rootstocks for grafting sweet orange, mandarin, grape fruit etc. On account of its vigorous growth and disease resistant qualities the sour orange serves as a good rootstock.

Commercial cultivation of sour orange is largely centred in the district of Guntur in Andhra Pradesh. This species includes a large number of varieties, some of them have originated as hybrids. The varietal traits are distinct in the shape, size and taste. In some varieties the outside of the petals is purple in colour. This is attributed to the hybridization with lemon. The variety *'Karna'* or *'Id nimbu'* is one of such hybrids. Its fruits resemble the sour orange but the flowers are tinged with purple as in lemon. Fruits are large, round and warty. The rind and pulp are orange in colour.

C. *aurantium* is grown sparsely, only in some places commercially. The plant is vigorous and thrives in any agricultural soil. Propagation is mainly by seed. But to avoid variation through sexual propagation the best forms are propagated by air layering or bud grafting.

The seedlings grow rapidly in rich soil. Flowering does not take place until the top is much-branched. To effect this the top shoots should be pinched off when the plant is 12 cm high. Generally it takes 4-6 years for flowering. But the plants propagated vegetatively yield much earlier.

The sour orange is now cultivated widely in Europe for its flowers and fruits. Orange flowers have an aesthetic value in a flower garden. The trees come into blossoms in abundance in February and March in the plains. In some areas second crop is also obtained in the early rains. The sweet fragrance is perceptible from a considerable distance.

Unlike sweet varieties the sour orange is strongly disease resistant. For this reason it does not fall victim to the killer diseases of the citrus family. It attains a great age in some parts of Spain. It is said that the surviving oldest plant is 600 years old.

In France, however, the seedlings are grafted with the scions collected from older and high yielding trees. This practice not only ensures early flowering but high yields also without losing desired varietal characters. Seedlings are not grafted in the early stage. They are usually reared in pots for three years and then transplanted in ground and grafted in the following year.

Tuberose (*Polyanthes tuberosa*)

In this country tuberose is grown extensively to meet the demand of the cut-flower market. It is, unfortunately, not exploited in perfumery. For its large-scale culture see 'Commercial culture of fragrant flowers for cut-flower trade'.

3

Cut-Flower Trade

The commercial floriculture or cut-flower business is expanding rapidly in our country. Prophet Mohammad has preached "If thou hast a loaf of bread sell half and buy the flowers of narcissus; for the bread nourisheth the body, but the narcissus the soul" (Crawford). The flowers are symbolic of beauty, love and tranquillity. The message of man's heart is best conveyed by flowers. Hence it is customary since ancient times till today to use flowers to send messages of love, joy and affection. It is said that one is born with flowers and dies with them. Really we cannot do anything without flowers. On all occasions well and woe, ritual or social, of love and honour, of glory or glamour offering, using or wearing of flowers is customary.

Previously flowers were purchased mainly for buyers' aesthetic appreciation, but today it is mainly for other reasons. Cut flowers especially the fragrant ones have various uses. Offering scented flowers to gods and goddesses is customary. Housewife with a vase of good flowers can aptly reveal her aesthetic appreciation. Ikebana is no more the monopoly of the Japanese. The art is widely practised at homes as well as displayed in the shows. Bridal decoration with scented flowers in our country is remarkable. In decorations in connection with festive occasions the role of flowers is very important. For the personal adornment of ladies the fragrant flowers are given preference. Hair decorations with white scented flowers are much more extensive in the southern states.

The presentation of bouquets and garlands to VIPs or to the loved ones is very common in our social behaviour. 'Say it with flowers' is wisely followed when a rich presentation with a large attractive bouquet is sent to *Sahib* or *Mem Sahib* on the occasion of new year's day to keep the boss or powerful officer in good humour. A victorious man is more befittingly congratulated with flowers. An ailing man expects congratulations with flowers from his friends and relatives on his recovery. Hearty sendoffs with floral tributes sweeten the pangs of separation. Cordial homage is paid to the departed soul with flowers. Flowers with bright gay looks and sweet perfume lighten the agony and gloominess happened to hang over the surroundings.

Not only the mortal beings the Heavens also have their weakness for the earthly flowers. Perhaps for this reason gods and goddesses are offered best flowers in accordance with their individual preference. *Durga* likes lotus preferably of blue colour. *Kali* is worshiped with red hibiscus. *Saraswati* is offered white flowers with sweet fragrance preferably the tuberose. *Vishnu* is pleased with Champa (*M. Champaca*) while *Vishnu* and *Lakshmi* together are fond of lotus. Ganesh is happy with yellow *Karavi* (*T. neriifolia*). *Datura* and *Akanda* (*Calotropis*) are the only flowers that are liked by *Mahakal* (The Lord of Eternity).

Every individual amongst us has his/her personal liking of flowers. Greatmen, too, are not the exception. Rabindra Nath Tagore longed for Bakul (*M. elengi*). Ramkrishna Deva was very fond of Nagkeshar (*Mesua ferrea*). Pandit Jawaharlal Nehru was always with a red rose on his third button hole.

Flowers are also used extensively to honour the dead souls. The mortal remains and the tombs are covered with flowers and flowers. On the occasion of any death anniversary the portraits or statues are garlanded and burial places are covered with wreaths of flowers and ornamental foliage. Flower offering is one of the most popular social customs. As much as 80 per cent of all flowers sold are used to pay homage to the deceased, as garlands and decorations at weddings and other festive occasions, as cheering gifts and token for congratulations, as expressions of thanks and love to hostesses, friends and beloveds. Hence the flower power is so extensive that a lot can be achieved with flowers.

BOOSTING PRODUCTION AND MARKETING

To augment the research work on agro-technique and breeding of commercially potential flowers Indian Council of Agricultural Research has set up a co-ordinated project. The project has taken up fourteen flowers. The rose, jasmine and tuberose are some of them. To assess the progress of the different research schemes the project holds a workshop at a few years' interval. The new techniques and cultivars developed by the technologists working under this project are transferred to the market growers and florists through the workshops.

Amongst the fragrant flowers the rose, jasmine and tuberose occupy a significant position in the cut-flower trade in India. The tuberose is largely produced and marketed near Calcutta and Bangalore, the jasmine in the south and the rose in the north. The up-to-date statistics on acreage, production and marketing are scanty.

EXPORT OF INDIAN FLOWERS

During the winter of 1978-79 flowers, seeds and ornamental plants worth around rupees one crore were exported to U.S.A., U.K., U.S.S.R., Japan and West Germany. Finland, Denmark, Norway and Switzerland are among the high per capita consuming countries of the world. The medium per capita consumption-level countries are Italy, France, Austria and Belgium, and the low per capita consumption-level countries are the U.K., Spain, Greece and Portugal (Mukherjee, B. 1982). Rose and carnation imported from non-European countries in 1978-79 were above 50 per cent of the total value of cut-flowers. The rose being the most favourite commodity in the cut-flower trade occupies the top position in the commercial floriculture. It is legendary. Perhaps it is the rose that is known to one and all.

Packaging and transportation of the perishables like flowers pose a major problem in a developing country like India towards exporting flowers to global markets. AGREXO extends its services towards gradation, storage and transportation of flowers. Special packaging methods have been prescribed by I.I.P. Innovations as to improved packaging will be warmly welcomed. The distance between the producing and consuming centres being far and wide delay in transporting deteriorates the quality of the commodity that does not go in favour of facing the keen competition of the foreign market. There is no direct air-links between the major cities of India and overseas flower markets. The IIFT has recommended to introduce air transportation schedules between our major cities and international airports. This organisation has also suggested to provide the facility of cold storage at the airports, which will save this perishable commodity in case of much delayed or temporarily suspended flights.

Flowers, like most commodities, face a crisis of keen competition in the international market. The marketable standard (export quality) of flowers must be attained at a moderate growing cost. Facilities of quick transportation of commodities from the growing areas to the marketing centres have to be achieved as a must. The countries which have succeeded in earning foreign exchange from flowers have primarily fulfilled these prerequisites. The reduced air freight for perishable goods like flowers and green vegetables is a necessity. Recently the reduction in freight upto ten per cent of the normal rates has been introduced for exporting flowers. The Ministry of Agriculture of the Central Government has announced on 16th November 1993 that the necessary infrastructure facilities will be available within a couple of years to export highly perishable commodities like vegetables and flowers. Columbia, Kenya, Singapore and Israel are the chief flower exporting countries. In exporting rose Israel tops the list. Every morning four planes are fully loaded with rose for Aalsmeer (Netherlands). The rose is not grown there outdoors. In the controlled condition of computerised greenhouses roses are planted 15-20 cm apart. The automatic system applies irrigation water, fertilizer, plant protection chemicals in the required doses as determined by the computer, thus saving labour to a great extent. Israel being an exporter of rose poses to be the main competitor of India. To have a success in this arena what we need is to originate the competent varieties to suit the taste of the market as well as that of consumers, in addition there should be improved technology, large investment and other infrastructure facilities.

WHOLESALE MARKET

The wholesale European market at Aalsmeer (Netherlands) is a distinct marketing channel through which flowers are passing from wholesale dealers to retail florists by auction. Flowers from the different growing centres of the world arrive at the big auction market during the night preceding the auction. This auction market is very interesting. Flowers are wheeled before the buyers sitting in the salesroom. The lot number and the description of flowers are then informed. Price bidding and recording are done by a mechanised method.

There is a single-hand indicator clock which is fixed at the highest price and its hand is moved towards the lower prices by the auctioneer. The first bidder has to push the button on his table to stop the arm of the clock. The price offered by him is recorded instantly with the lot number of the flowers. Money transfer takes place immediately from buyer's account to that of the seller. Then the next lot of flowers has to be auctioned. The whole operation of moving flowers from the grower's field to consumer's bag takes place within 24-48 hours through the wholesale market. Frankfurt (Germany) being another wholesale market for cut-flowers. Besides many countries despatch their flowers straightway to the big florists of the consumer countries.

GROWING FLOWERS FOR EXPORT TRADE

Apparently growing flowers may seem to be a luxury in our developing countries where most of the people are struggling hard for bare necessities. But the cut-flowers have a good market both at home and abroad, as such, flower growing has a good employment potential for the millions of our country.

The annual sale of cut-flowers in America is of 1.50 billion dollars. Germany being the largest importer of cut-flowers which cost around 50 million dollars. Israel grows rose for the European market in glasshouses in K. Mozra. Kenya earns 10 crores of rupees by exporting flowers. Malaysia and Thailand export orchid flowers to foreign markets. India has a wide scope of earning foreign exchange by exporting flowers. At present Germany is the largest importer of Indian flowers. The demand of flowers in the European market rises in winter when they have to grow flowers in greenhouses. A wide range of climatic conditions prevails in hills and plains of India, which favours the growing of almost all kinds of flowers belonging to temperate and tropical zones.

Secondly a particular type of flowers can be harvested throughout the year if grown in the plains during winter and in the hills during summer. The cost of production of flowers is cheaper in India as compared to the developed countries of Europe where the cost of labour or farm mechanization is very high. The prices of flowers are much higher in foreign markets than those prevailing in this country. The prices of flowers sold in Delhi during winter are as follows: carnations at Rs. 10-12, roses Rs. 12-24 and tuberose spikes Rs. 6-9 per dozen.

POST-HARVEST CARE

Flower crops after harvest demand very careful and scientific handling for prolonging their life. Either from a home garden or from the commercial field flowers are required for decoration purposes and as such keeping quality thereof is of vital importance. The fundamental processes related to the keeping quality are water absorption, transpiration and respiration.

Packaging: Packaging of flowers is not only concerned with the convenience of transporting but also preserving them in a good condition so that their freshness is retained for a long time. Respiration, transpiration and rate of cell division are directly related to life processes of cut flowers. The practice relating to the maintenance of life of cut flowers must account for the action and interaction of these processes, which must be on the low ebb for long storage life and keeping quality. To accomplish this a package should have a small volume; it must be gas-proof, non-absorbent of water and sufficiently strong to resist any pressure during transit.

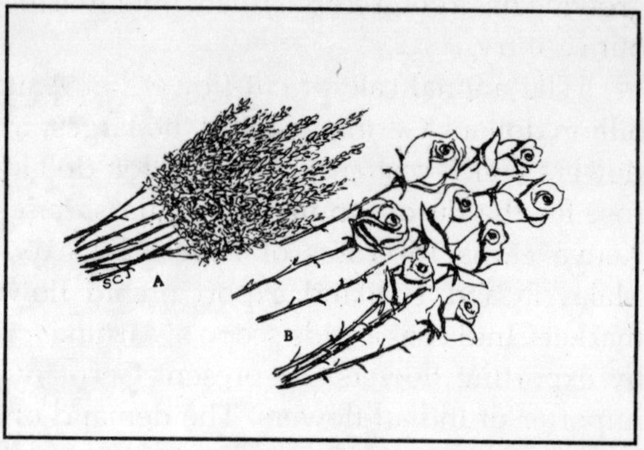

CUT-FLOWERS
A. Spikes of Tuberose
B. H.T. Roses with Stems (30 cm Long)

The blooms with stems of the required length are wrapped with polythene film and placed in paper-board cartons. This can satisfy the need of small volume in the package space, excessive humidity and gas and waterproof condition. The rate of transpiration is lowered due to the accumulation of carbon dioxide in the packing. As the cut stems cannot perform the normal absorption the deficiency of water within the tissues occurs resulting in the low rate of cell division.

An extremely scented single-flowered Sambac originated by the author, through selection from Seedlings

A variegated form of P. Odoratissimus (Above left)

← Coroupita Guianensis
Courtesy: Sunil Kumar Dey

Author's Rose Garden (At Jhargram, Midnapur)

Originating New Roses. Ten-week old Rose Seedlings Raised in Horticultural Arena in January 1994.

Honey Bee on a Perfumed Rose

From garden to the market: Cutting, handling, pre-cooling and packaging are the operations that are involved in sending flowers to the market. Flowers being soft and tender a special care is needed to present the commodity to the customers in a garden-fresh condition. They should be cut at a right stage of growth. Immediately after cutting the cut-ends of the stems must be put under water of a bucket. After harvesting the crop is brought under a shed when the stems are stripped of foliage and thorns if any. The stem is cut again (at least few millimetres) under water of a container, which will remove the air from the cut surface. To improve the keeping quality 'hardening' of buds becomes necessary. For this purpose the flowers with their stems are preserved for 8-12 hours at an air temperature of 40°F. After this operation the flowers are sorted out, and the selected ones are packed in a paper-board carton. This process is followed in case of rose blooms before air shipment to foreign markets. But the method of handling flowers for an inland market is different. The growers are not so meticulous for a longer life of their flowers. Although flowers are cut in their right stage of opening the necessity of removing leaves and thorns from the stems, pre-cooling and even putting the stems into water is not felt. Simply the flowers have a bath in water for a few minutes; then they are taken out and held with flower heads downward to drain off excess water, and put into a simple packing of polythene film and hessian cloth. It should be borne in mind that a large quantity of flowers huddled up in a packing does travel well but many petals get bruised to some extent. Secondly fermentation is likely to take place if flowers are kept in such packings for more than six hours in a rising day temperature. A special type of basket for a limited quantity of flowers should be devised for carrying flowers to the market.

Flowers get a longer life in a cold weather. On the contrary, in hot weathers they are highly perishable. A hot dry weather is definitely worse than a hot humid one. This is why cut flower markets in the open along the coastal line of India carry on their business quite well in summer. During summer only the fragrant flowers reign supreme in the market. Because tuberose and the different types of jasmine become chief commodities.

This flower market must be in a shed or it will shorten the life of flowers. But it is surprising how people are buying and selling flowers quite well in a hot mid-day sun in the open flower market at Jagannath Ghat near Howrah Bridge (now Rabindra Setu). This is possible only because of excess humidity in the atmosphere on the bank of the river Hooghly. The sellers are found to prefer an open sunny place which, I presume, makes their flowers brighter. A wholesale flower market is a brisk market. In the morning with bright sunshine colourful commodities like flowers look fresher and brighter; and attract the buyers instantly. As the day advances they have to resort to sprinkling of water to cope with the heat of the day. From the wholesale market flowers go to the florist shops where utmost care is taken to lengthen the life of flowers and as such they are placed in glass cases both for preservation and displaying. Cut flowers can be placed in a freezing condition for a week or so. Although petals do not wither staleness however develops with change of colours.

Improved cultural techniques are also involved in regard to the life of cut flowers. The use of excessive nitrogenous fertilizer in comparison with phosphate and potassic ones makes the tissues of petals soft. Naturally such produce does not last longer. To illustrate this the tuberose grown in West Bengal may be cited. In two growing areas the cultural techniques are different. The growers of Kolaghat area of Midnapur use only organic manure like cow-manure, hoof and hornmeal, bonemeal, mustard cake, etc. But at Purnanagar (near Ranaghat, Nadia) in growing tuberose organic manures are supplemented with large amount of chemical fertilizers. The floral produce of Kolaghat fetches a better price on account of the high keeping quality than that of Ranaghat. Hence the growers should pay more attention to use plenty of manures supplemented with a little quantity of fertilizer.

Vase life of cut flowers: Efforts are made to lengthen the vase life of cut flowers. But it is dependent on many factors related to the maintenance of proper conditions conducive to the life of a flower. One should be careful to the stage of opening of the particular species/variety of flowers to be picked for this purpose. Because fully open flowers usually have a short life. Flowers picked at the early stage of opening are best. The flowers like roses, gardenias etc. last longer in a vase if picked when the outer petals have just started opening. In case of inflorescence like tuberose, coroupita etc. the flowering shoots should be cut when a few basal buds have opened. Flowers should be picked early in the morning or at sundown. Use a sharp cutting knife or secateurs. While cutting make a slanting cut to increase the water absorbing surface. Immediately after cutting the flower stalks or stems should be immersed into the water of a bucket; and then be transferred to the vase. Water ascends mainly through the cut end. But the process gets interrupted if a film of air covers the cells of the cut surface. To get rid of the trouble cut down the base of the stems (at least few millimetres) under the water of the bucket, that will keep off air to be present at the cut surface. Although in lesser amount the whole surface of the stems is capable of absorbing water. Hence a long stalked flower dipped upto its neck in the vase water does not normally flag in want of sap. The water of the container should preferably be changed on alternate days, where the stem ends be re-cut to facilitate the ascent of water.

The use of certain chemical compounds in the vase water is believed to increase the life span of flowers. The principle therein being to slow down the respiration of flowers, that delays ageing. Proprietary preparations of such compounds are marketed in various trade names: 'Bloom life', Floralife', Sta-fresh etc. As most of them are foreign products, so one can hardly be able to procure them from our markets. A user may also prepare his compound by following the formula which can be used for prolonging the life of vase blooms.

(i)	Alum	1/4 teaspoonful
(ii)	Sodium hypoclorite (Clorix)	1/4 teaspoonful
(iii)	Sugar	2 teaspoonful
(iv)	Water	One quart

The use of sugar, common salt or aspirin is in vogue for this purpose. 4 per cent sugar solution is generally recommended in the vase water for tuberose.

Obviously too warm condition of a room is not suitable for vase flowers. Flowers wither quickly if breeze or wind blows over them. Thirdly in a humid weather, for obvious reasons, flowers last longer. Hence glass show-cases are used for keeping flowers in the florist's shop for controlling environmental factors. The experiments in the laboratory have proved that rose buds if treated with ethylene gas last longer in the vase. In this process the buds that have just started opening should be treated with 25 per cent ethylene gas for 24 hours. The petals of the bloom thus treated will be opening slowly. The buds of different cultivars, however, need different amounts of gas. If the percentage of gas exceeds 3 per cent of the buds will turn brown and will never open. A special type of apparatus is required for applying the gas. Because the gas is harmful to human beings.

Under All India Co-ordinated Floricultural Improvement Project the research works were conducted in Ganeshkhind (Pune) to find out the means to lengthen the vase life of roses. It has been found out there that the use of aluminium sulphate, sugar and Bavistin is very useful. The following table will show the specific utility of the different materials used in the experiments.

The results of the experiments with different materials to lengthen the vase life of roses

Sl. No.	Chemicals	Longevity (days)	Rate of opening petals	Water absorbed (ml)	Drooping
1.	Without water	0.50	4.60	—	10.00
2.	Water	2.50	3.62	28.87	10.00
3.	Water + Bavistin 0.1%	6.25	3.05	19.62	4.00
4.	Water + sucrose 3.0%	3.50	4.00	48.87	7.25
5.	Water + sucrose 3.0% + aluminium sulphate (500 ppm)	7.00	3.10	41.37	4.00
6.	Water + sucrose 3.0% + citric acid (500 ppm)	6.75	3.62	40.75	5.75

Time of experiments	17 August, 1987
Length of stalks	60 cm
Size and condition of buds	Just opening, diameter 5-7 cm
Cultivar	Gladiator (Toro)
Number of flowers	10
Number of experiments	4

FLOWERS FOR THE MARKET

Rose

The rose being the most favourite commodity in the cut-flower trade occupies the top position in the commercial floriculture. It is legendary. Perhaps it is the rose that is known to one and all.

The trading with cut roses begins in the days of Pharaoh when Egypt shipped roses to Rome. It is said that the Greeks learned the uses of the rose from Egyptians. Nowadays all countries have their own farming and marketing for their internal consumption. And some countries grow roses with a special care adopting the modern technology for exporting. The developing countries like Columbia, Kenya, Singapore,

Israel, etc. earn a lot of foreign exchange through exporting roses. The quality of flowers of the internal market of the developing countries and that of the wholesale market of Europe are not same. In the wholesale market there is a keen competition as to the quality of blooms. Gradually the standard of quality rises; and to attain this many features of the modern technology are being exploited. For roses greenhouse culture has become a standard practice. Because flowers grown outdoors cannot be at par with those of indoor qualitatively and quantitatively. The high percentage of blooms raised indoors attains the quality as demanded by the more sophisticated markets of the world. In other words, to achieve the quality, computerised greenhouse practice has become imperative. Those countries which export roses have developed their own competent varieties through breeding. A number of good qualities, such as elegant form, slow opening, sweet fragrance, pleasant colour etc., must be combined in one variety to be qualified as a good export-quality strain. Such varieties are hardly found among the general cultivated varieties. Hence the necessity of breeding competent varieties. Any variety hardly possesses all the qualities of a good bloom. For this reason efforts are directed to originate new varieties having as many as those qualities which are of pleasant colour and medium size, elegant form and sweet fragrance, strong and stately stalks, stems with less thorn and more buds, and flowers with a slow opening habit and long vase life.

Besides an easy growing habit with less care and plant-protection measure is also wanted. All India Co-ordinated Floricultural Improvement Project laid emphasis on originating new varieties suitable for cut flowers in its 5th Workshop, as such the research work in this direction had been taken up in Indian Agricultural Research Institute (New Delhi) under ICAR.

India, like the advanced countries, should introduce the Plant Patent Act to safeguard the interest of the breeders. And this will attract the breeders and ensure the flow of funds from the private sector for intensive as well as extensive works.

The varieties which own the export qualities and are exported from India are not many. The top ten amongst the large-flowered varieties are 'Sonia Meilland' (Salmon Pink), 'Ilona' (Red), 'Red Success' (Red), 'Baccara' (Vermilion red), 'Lamenuette' (White with reddish margin), 'Aalsmeer Gold' (Golden yellow), 'Cocktail-60' (Yellow), 'Diana' (Yellow), 'Prive' (Orange red) and 'Carlita' (Pink).

In our country first computerised greenhouse has been set up in Bangalore for growing roses for export. Its owner All-India Scheduled Castes Cooperative Society has taken up the venture in foreign collaboration for fund and technology. This greenhouse of 100 acres has been claimed to be the largest of its kind in the world. To make the project a success the international wholesale market of Netherlands has placed an order of 20 crores of rupees for supplying flowers in the first year. The Statesman, an English daily of Calcutta, highlights the matter in 1991, which is as follows.

"Computerised glass house

Hyderabad, June 7 (UNI): The world's largest computerised "glass house" to monitor climatic conditions of different varieties of high-value flowers meant for export is fast coming up on a 100-acre site near Bangalore.

A Netherland-based bank is funding the Rs. 100 crore-glass house. Mr. Yogendra Makwana, president of the All-India Scheduled Castes Development Cooperative Society, told reporters here yesterday. He said the necessity for setting up this modern facility arose because of the growing international trade in flowers. Three billion dollars worth trade takes place every year in the international flower market at Amsterdam in Netherlands, but India's flower exports were negligible, he added.

Mr. Makwana said India had entered the international market by bagging a Rs. 20 crore order in Netherlands, to be executed within a year. The order was won by the 'Vegetable and Flower Farm' of the All-India Scheduled Castes Development Cooperative Society, at Kunigal in Karnataka.

The first consignment is likely to be airfreighted in October this year."

For growing outdoors as much as 10,000 rose bushes can be grown in an acre of land. The production rises to 50,000 export quality blooms, i.e., 5 blooms per bush on an average during the winter months. At the end of the last decade Indian roses were quoted a price range of Rs. 18 to 24 per doz or Rs. 150 per 100 blooms in Frankfurt market during winter. No crop other than roses has such a good market. But the market price is quite remunerative in Germany and Switzerland.

Orchid

Orchid is an excellent cut flower for its qualities of long lasting, regal form, attractive colour and pleasant aroma. The entire flower spike or the individual flower has its use as a cut-flower. The spike is used in different floral decorations while a single flower is used in button holes. An orchid button hole lends an air of distinction to the wearer; hence its use being a fashion.

Since orchids last longer than any other flower its demand in the cut-flower trade is gradually increasing. Most flowers when required for distant markets are cut in a particular stage of the bud which is about to open. Because open flowers have usually a shorter life. But this rule does not apply in case of orchid. The flowers in a bud stage or even in their opening stage are not good. Only the fully open matured flowers last longer after cutting.

Cut the flowers early in the morning or in the evening. The cut end of the spike should be immediately placed in water. The cut surface must be greater in area to absorb more water. This can be done by cutting it slantwise. Air bubbles clung to the surface prevent passage of water through the cells. Hence it is better to give a final cut at the base of the spike holding it under water.

Double Tuberose Cv. Pearl

Strongly Fragrant Rose Cv. 'Double Delight' (Above left)

← Strongly Fragrant Rose Cv. 'Paradise'

Strongly Fragrant Rose Cv. 'Martin Luther King'

Strongly Fragrant Roses, Cvs. "Paradise" (Top), 'Papa Meilland' (Below right), 'Super Star' (Below left)

Fragrant varieties: A series of observations were made by a French botanist E. Andre to find out the scented varieties of the orchid. The following includes some of his findings.

Although the breeders have originated innumerable fantastic orchids sweetly scented varieties are very limited. A good number of them are as follows:

Acropera ioddigeii, Angraceum fatuosum, Bifrenaria indora, Catasetum scurra, Cattleya eldorado, Caeliopsis hyacithesma, Cleistoma ionasmum, Dendrobium glumaceum, Dendrobium nobile, Epidendrum vulnerum, Macillaria aromatica, Odontoglossum citrosum, Odontoglossum gloriosum, Orchis sambucina, Zygopetalum mackayi, Herminium monorchis, Haboenaria conopsea, Cymbiium ensifolium, Cattleya citrina (Lime scent), Cattleya intermedia (Musk scent), Cattleya custata (Banana-coconut scent), Cattleya massangeana, Cattleya speciosa, Cymbidium simulance (from Sikkim), Cymbidium eburneum, Cymbidium ensifolium, Dendrobium aggregatum (honey scent), Dendrobium chrysotoxum, Dendrobium devonianum, Dendrobium moschatum (musk scent), Odontoglossum pendulum (rose scented), Vanda cristata, Vanda tricolour, Vanda suavis, etc.

It is interesting to note that in some orchids odour changes with the diurnal phase. For example *Dendrobium nobile* emits odour of primrose in the morning, honey at noon and hay in the evening.

Tuberose

Amongst the fragrant flowers tuberose and jasmines occupy a very prominent place in the fresh-flower trade. Delightfully fragrant flowers of tuberose remain fresh for a pretty long time. Moreover, tuberose stands transportation to distant markets. The vase life of a tuberose spike varies from 6-12 days depending upon the care taken and the temperature and humidity of the surrounding. Hence its extensive popularity.

The flowers open in the dusk, as such it has a brisk local market in the evening. Exuberance of delicious fragrance of freshly open flowers attracts young people tremendously. The mature buds are plucked in the afternoon and after putting them on a string they are packed in baskets with sufficient moisture. The buds open nicely with strong perfume when unpacked in the evening market.

In Calcutta, Bangalore, Bombay and Pune the cut-flower markets abound in tuberose. The whole spikes with few open flowers and plenty of buds of all sizes are sold in bundles. Loose flowers are also available by weight and also in form of garlands for various decorations. For the distant markets flowers are cut and tied into bundles. In the large fields flowers are picked by women and child labour on contract at the rate of 50-75 paise per kg. Loose flowers are packed in baskets and the bundles of spikes are wrapped with cloth (cotton or hessian). In Calcutta the largest whole-sale flower market being 'Jagannath Ghat' on the bank of the river Hooghly. It starts from 8 A.M. Heaps of flowers are poured in which cover the entire space. The florists from the different parts come over there for their floral purchase. Hawker florists give a better price for the fresh bundles of tuberose for selling them at Dum Dum airport where air-passengers collect them avidly as they are very costly in their places.

Artificial colouring: All varieties of tuberose are white. There is no attractive colour variation. Florists and flower lovers desire to have flowers in different colours and shades. Unfortunately tuberose being monotype intraspecific hybridization has been ineffective to bring about a change in colour. Even mutation breeding (treated with Gamma rays) has failed to induce any colour-break. A change has however been effected in leaves which have got white streaks. Hence florists have devised to induce colours to tuberose flowers through the chemical means.

Previously eosin was added to the water of a flask in which tuberose spikes were dipped for 30-60 minutes. The solution ascended through the stems resulting in the colour change of the petals. Nowadays a number of chemicals of different colours have been introduced for this purpose. Bromocresol Green, Bromophenol Blue, Phenol Red,

Erythrosin Red, Ammonium purpurate and Eosin have been tried with good results. By changing the concentration of the chemical the shades of induced colour can be altered. The flower stalks are dipped in the solution of the chemical for 30-60 minutes. The different concentrations such as 0.25%, 0.05%, 0.075%, 0.1% and 0.2% may be used. After colouring the stalks are taken out of the solution and kept in a bucket of fresh water. Although the florists of the sophisticated markets use chemicals for inducing different colours and shades the wayside vendors are in favour of soothing bluish tinge. Nicely blue hued tuberose sold in the afternoon near the Howrah Rly Station bears testimony to this statement. The flowers of *J. auriculatum* and *J. sambac* are also induced with light blue tinge.

Jasmine (*J. sambac*)

The double-flowered forms (Motiya, Moti bel, Gundumalli) are most popular. They are cultivated on a commercial scale in Uttar Pradesh (at Kanauj, Jaunpur, Ghazipur and Sikandarpur), West Bengal (Midnapur and Howrah) and Tamil Nadu. The average yield of flowers per acre is 700 kg-1000 kg. Each flower weighs 300-400 mg, thus 1 kg of flowers counts 3000-4000. In the big cities of India about 1000 kg of sambac is sold every day. Gradually the production is increasing to meet the growing demand of the flower.

The buds of sambac are in great demand in the fresh flower market of India. Strongly scented garlands of white beads of sambac buds are fascinating to ladies for hair decorations and ornaments. Large buds are picked and sold. One plant may yield about 500 grams of buds in a season. Sambac garlands are sold by hawkers in the evening market, temple premises, parks etc. They attract the fanciers greatly in the evening when they emit sweet perfume.

Jasmine (*J. auriculatum*)

The small bead-like buds are picked in the afternoon and used in making garlands. Jui buds are very useful in making floral ornaments which have a great demand for bridal decoration. For this reason, in the marriage season Jui fetches a good price.

Kewda (*P. odoratissimus*)

For scenting the air of a room kewda spadices are used as vase flowers. The perfume comes from the spathes, the greenish white leaves covering the inflorescence. Roxburgh says, "It is the tender white leaves of the flowers, chiefly of the male, that yield the most delightful fragrance for which they are so universally and deservedly esteemed. For of all perfumes in world it must be the richest and most powerful."

As a cut flower its demand is so heavy in the rural Bengal that one hardly finds them in the city trade centres. Its demand in the industrial area has extremely increased.

In 1980 the author made a survey on its price in the different bazaars of the district of Midnapur where the flowers (male spadix) were sold at paise fifty each. In the industrial areas of Bihar they were sold at Rs. 1.50-2.00 each.

At present times no mature spadix is available in the market. Only immature flowers with less perfume are available. As they are collected from the natural vegetation of fallow lands a keen competition among the flower pickers is found; as a consequence the flowers are picked before attaining maturity.

Champaka (*M. champaca*)

It is one of the most popular flowers of India. The production is sufficient in Orissa, Andhra Pradesh, Tamil Nadu, Kerala and Karnataka. In North Bengal afforestation with *Champaka* has been taken up by the Government Forest Department. *Champaka* is much favoured by the South Indian people. To meet the demand of those people living in Calcutta *Champaka* is brought to the city from Tamil Nadu by air. The commercial production of *Champaka* is also found in Ranaghat in the district of Nadia. Kharagpur, the railway town, has a good population of Telegu people, where florists collect flowers (*M. champaca*) from a nearby town of Jhargram to meet the demand from the Telegu people.

Champaka attar is produced in Paralakhemundi in the district of Gajapathi (formerly Ganjam).

SCENTED FLOWERS FOR FLOWER ARRANGING AND VASE DECORATION

Kadamba (*A. cadamba*): The flower heads are used for decoration on festive occasions. They are available in June and July.

Hasu-na-hana (*C. nocturnum*): For its fragrance alone shoots with mature inflorescence are cut in the evening and put in the flower vase. It sweetens the air of the room with intense perfume all over the night.

No work has been done to investigate the nature and quality of the essential oil content of Hasu-na-hana. It is probably due to its reduced corolla.

Nagalingam (*C. guianensis*): The flowers and inflorescence of *nagalingam* are considered unique objects for ikebana. The flowers are prized for offering to deities in temples. As a cut flower *nagalingam* has a good demand in the local markets. It has no use in perfumery.

Mehndi (*L. inermis*): Flowering shoots of mehndi are put in vases together with the ornamental foliage of other plants. The perfume from the vase flowers sweetens the air of the room.

Plumeria: As the flowers are very beautiful, fragrant and long lasting, they are used for making garlands. A garland of plumeria may remain fresh for several days. In dry areas where flowers are very costly in summer plumerias as cut flowers may be the answer. A very floriferous variety "APURVA" (developed by the author) should be selected for this purpose.

Kamini (*Murraya paniculata*): Although short lived is highly prized for its strong sweet perfume. Shoots with mature buds are cut in the evening and put in the vase. Then its perfume spreads in the room.

Gardenia: 'Flower vendors are on hand to greet the tourist in Madeira (an Atlantic island). Fragrant gardenias and exotic orchids are often tossed into the lap of a delighted visitor who hastily throws back a coin from his car to his trusting salesman' (Lands and People).

But in this country it is not found in the trade. Perhaps only the housewives use it in the vase mainly for its strong sweet perfume.

Nyctanthes (*N. arbor-tristis*): The flowers being highly perishable and delicate are used before noon, mainly for offering to deities and making garlands. Repeated handling damages the petals quickly. So the flowers need a soft careful handling in their collection and use.

4

Essential Oil Industry

One of the ancient uses of perfume was man's offering of pleasant spicy odours to gods by the burning of incense and hence the word perfume derives from the Latin *perfumus* meaning 'through smoke'.

FLOWER PERFUME AND PERFUMERY

In 4th century B.C. the interest in the essential oil was developed in India, Egypt and Persia. Fats and oils were used in ancient Greece and Rome to extract perfume oil from roots and flowers. From the fall of Rome to Renaissance perfumery was mainly nurtured by the hands of the Arabs and the Persians who built up an important foreign trade on perfumery articles. During the Renaissance a fresh interest was awakened in perfumery in France and Italy. From the 17th century scientific investigations began to explore essential oils and their method of extraction. Towards the end of the 18th century the extraction of flower perfume became an industry in France. In the beginning a flower water prepared from orange flower was introduced by the Duchess of Neroli. This flower water owes its name to Neroli. Since then it is known as 'Neroli'. Neroli is an important ingredient of eau-de-cologne which was introduced by J.M. Farnia around 1725. This cologne however becomes more floral types by the middle of the last century. And it is then the fancy of sophisticated perfumes of France made their appearance. In the early stage they were based on the oils of Vanilla, Vetiver, Patchouli etc. Before the beginning of this century perfumery got a greater variety of odour effects on account of the discovery of synthetic chemicals for the substitution of natural oils. Generally the taste for heavy flowery notes was modified with amyl (isoamyl) salicylate and methyl noyl acetaldehyde. Although it is still popular the use of sandalwood, vetiver, musk and civet has been increased in compounding.

Like other fancy articles different countries have developed their own taste as regards perfume. Lavender, rose and 'lily of the valley' are popular in Great Britain. Hyacinth and lilac in Netherlands. Powdery notes of vanillin, orris, opopanax, etc. are preferred by the French fashion houses, whereas Spain and South America have their liking for spicy notes. But the United States prefers ones that are based on the heavy exotic flower idiom.

VOLATILE PERFUME OIL

Perfume oil which is also known as essential oil, contained in the floral parts is volatile. Different flowers yield different types of oil. Not only that their qualities also vary. Rose, *Kewda*, jasmine are the important flowers from which perfume oil is extracted in this country. Tuberose though produced in the largest quantity and its oil content is also high is not employed in oil extraction in India. *Champaka* (*M. champaca*) oil is extracted on a very limited scale. The oil content of the different flowers is as follows: Rose .06%, Jasmine .03%, *Kewda* 0.3%, *Champaka* 0.3% and Orange 0.6%.

ESSENCE OF NEROLI

In the history of perfumery it has been mentioned that in the 16th century the Italian philosopher Porta obtained an oil of exquisite fragrance by distilling citrus flowers. In 1680 the essential oil from orange blossoms was called essence of Neroli. The reason is attributed to the fact that it was used for perfuming garments by the wife of Flavio Orsine, Prince of Neroli.

In China orange flowers are collected when fully open and are used for scenting tea known as orange *Pekoe.* In the south of France orange trees are grown mainly for their flowers.

In India citrus oil is produced in East Khandesh (Maharashtra).

In France the production of flowers is recorded from 12-15 kilos per plant in a good year. The total crop exceeds 2 million kg per year. The perfume of orange flowers is both sweet and strong but those of bitter varieties have finer aroma which suggests jasmine slightly.

The oil extracted by distillation from orange blossoms is known as 'oil of neroli' and that by volatile solvent is 'orange flower absolute'. The yield of oil recorded in the south of France is 1500 grams for 1000 kg of flowers. In Tunis oil of neroli is produced by distillation which can compete well with the French product.

In Charabot and Lonone it has been found by experiments that dry flowers yield a higher percentage of oil than the fresh. Flowers collected in a fine weather of spring yield better than those of rainy season.

The process of distillation has always been employed for extraction of orange blossom oil as it yields much more than the other processes including the use of volatile solvents. The average yield being 900-1100 grams from 1000 kg of flowers. Previously orange flower water was considered as a significant by-product. But today it is much esteemed in commerce for its delightful fragrance of fresh blossoms. In perfumery of today neroli oil is considered a powerful ingredient.

The aqueous distillate from a distillation plant may be subjected to solvent extraction. In this novel process flower water is treated with volatile solvent like acetone, petroleum ether to extract the perfume. The product is very powerful, its odour is about ten times stronger than the normal oil.

The different grades of orange flower-water are sold in perfumery markets. Their gradation depends on oil content of the flower. Generally distillates are classified on this basis. The first part consisting of the four-fifths of the total water used contains more oil than the remaining one-fifth. The oil content of the first part has been found to be 0.031 per cent whereas the last part contains 0.008 per cent only. The cohobated water however contains much more oil (see Cohobation).

FLOWER OIL VERSUS SYNTHETIC OIL

To meet the excessive demand of perfume oil the modern chemical technology has succeeded in synthesising imitation oil. Because the production of natural oils from flowers is very limited, which cannot cope with the boisterous demand of perfumery and allied industries. The production cost of natural oil is much higher than synthetic oils. Hence the latter has gained popularity so far as its extensive use is concerned. In quality, however, the natural flower oil is inimitable in toto. To soften the tone of a synthetic oil one or more natural products are required. In preparing cosmetics of superior quality the use of natural products is required; as such the use of natural oils predominates.

ISOLATES

Isolates are active principles responsible for specific characters. In nature they occur in plant materials including flowers usually in combination with a.number of them. By applying chemical methods such as fractional distillation, molecular distillation, chilling etc., the active principles are isolated. Hence the term 'isolates'. The isolates are used as raw materials in making compounds for creating specific pleasing notes. Now isolates are being prepared synthetically. But those which are obtained from the natural sources are sweeter and more pleasing than the synthetics. The following is a list of common isolates which are regarded as perfumery aromatics:

Citral, Citronellol, Eugenol, Geraniol, Heliotropin, Hydroxy-citronellol, Ionones, Isoboryl acetate, Linalol, Linalyl acetate,.Menthol, Terpineols, Terpinyl acetate, Vanillin etc. etc.

COMPOUNDING AND COMPOUNDS OF PERFUMES

In perfumery two processes are involved: one is science that helps obtain raw materials either from natural sources or synthetic chemicals; other is art required to produce finished products by blending a number of selected materials in measured proportions in order to infuse a desirable note. It is not difficult to make out that the perfumes are extracted or synthesised by scientific techniques. But it may not be discernible to many how perfumery products are prepared by architectural or artistic skill. In order to illustrate it is compared to music or painting. In painting ideas are brought out by harmonizing colours, in music by harmonizing sounds, in perfumery by harmonizing odours through blending.

In painting, music and perfumery one common practice is to select a central exponent around which the concerto is developed. In such a practice emphasis is laid on one instrument in music, one colour in painting and one odour in perfumery.

A perfumer is necessarily an artist who must be aesthetically sensitive to select appropriate materials for his delightful creation. It is also true that such an artist should have a sound background of chemistry for his dynamic career. He has to be acquainted with the characters of thousands of raw materials as to be able to make critical assessment of their purity and to identify the bodies used in the complex blends.

Finished perfumes: Finished perfumes in alcoholic solutions are sold in attractive containers for use on handkerchief, dresses or bodies. They are commonly known as 'handkerchief perfumes'. A complicated mixture of odorous ingredients is mixed with alcohol and preserved for few months after which it is filtered and bottled. A handkerchief perfume usually contains 5% to 20% of essence and an eau-de-cologne 2%-10%. In expensive products tinctures (alcoholic solutions) of musk, ambergris etc. are used. They are very expensive and added towards the final stage of preparation.

Perfumers innovate formulas for specific floral notes in which the fragrance of a particular flower will predominate. The selection of the isolates for a particular formula and their ratio in the preparation add individuality to the product. The innovator concerned puts a specific name to each product to recognise them, such as Orchid No. 1052, Orchid No. 1053, Red Rose No. 1057 etc. Like other products the innovators of floral bouquets get their formulas patented.

Rose No. 001

Geraniol	75
Phenylethyl alcohol	65
Linalol	25
Rhodinol	25
Citronellol	10
Aldehyde C_9	1.5
Citral	0.5
	211

Rose No. 1050

Rose Otto (synthetic)	20
Rose Otto (Bulgaria)	2
Rose absolute	5
Rose compound	30
Jasmine absolute	2
Civet absolute	1
Musk tincture (3%)	50
Alcohol	600
	800

Tuberose No. 1055

Tuberose compound	100
Jasmine absolute	6
Gardenia compound	40
Orange flower absolute	4
Musk ticture (3%)	10
Alcohol	700
	860

Tuberose No. 001

Tuberose absolute	5
Jasmine absolute	1.5
Orange flower absolute	1.5

Musk tincture (3%)	2
Alcohol	50
	60

INDIAN PERFUMERY

In ancient times the art of perfumery in India had an established reputation in other countries. The account of many historic travellers bears testimony to this fact. The exquisite perfumes produced in India were marketed in Europe in medieval times under the name of Arabian perfumes. In those days the perfumery industry developed in Kanauj, Kumbakonam, Bangalore, Pandharpur, Poona and Patna. Since the Mughal periods Jaunpur, Ghazipur, Lucknow, Delhi and Aligarh have been producing floral perfumes of high quality. The perfumery articles were among the important commodities of trade that flourished in those days with the neighbouring countries. The patronage of the royal families and aristocracy helped in developing the industry.

In the context of the tremendous development of the chemical technology in the western world during the later half of the twentieth century the Indian perfumery industry has failed to keep pace in the race. At present researches are being carried on in the various research centres to mould the industry with the modern technology. The Indian floral perfumes are mainly available in the form of attar, hair oil and floral water.

The Indian industry of perfume extraction from flowers is entirely based on a cottage scale. Until very recently there is scarcely any production of flower oils and absolutes. The modern process of solvent extraction employed in a few firms in the south has enabled to produce jasmine concrete and absolute. Certain firms and institutes like Harcourt Butler Technological Institute (Kanpur), Tata Oil Mills Co. Ltd. (Bombay) etc. have produced jasmine and rose oil on an experimental scale. *Champaka* oil is also produced on a small scale from flowers of *Champaka* (*M. champaca*). The following firms are known to produce essential oils in this country:

Encee Ltd. (Mettupalayam), Tata Oil Mills Co. Ltd. (Bombay), Calcutta Chemical Co. Ltd. (Calcutta), Ghosh Brothers (Perfumer, Calcutta), Techno Chemical Ltd. (Kazhikode), Standard Essential Oil Distillers (Kanpur), Gupta & Co. (Delhi), Makhanlal Ramnarain and Banarasidas Khatri (Kanauj).

Attars are distillates collected over sandalwood oil, vetiver oil or similar other products. The quality of the *attar* obviously depends on the quality of oil available in the product. The more pleasing the flowery note the higher is its price. *Attars* used in the products includes—tobacco, hair oils, soaps, *Agarbattis* etc. Alcoholic solutions of *attar* which are now available have various uses. The centres of production of jasmine *attars* are Kanauj, Jaunpur, Ghazipur and Sikandarpur. For rose *attar* the centres are Ghazipur, Barwana and Husayan. Kewda *attar* is produced in Chhatrapur, Berhampur, Jagannathpur and Gopalpur in the district of Ganjam (Orissa). Although *Kewda* plants are distributed almost throughout India 90% of the production of Kewda flowers is estimated in this district of Orissa. Perfumery houses chiefly from U.P. send their representatives with distillation equipments to Ganjam for the spot distillation of Kewda oil during the flowering season. Nearly 2700 kg of *attar* of 20 different grades is prepared in U.P. every year.

Indian Attars: The fragrant flowers are subjected to water distillation for the preparation of *attars*. The vapours from the still are condensed and absorbed in sandalwood oil. Sandalwood oil free from lower terpenes is ideal for *attars* which enhances their mellowness and strikingly pleasant fragrant note. To remove those undesirable terpenes the base oil is washed with the end distillate from the previous batch. The concentration of the essential oil in the base oil is increased by the repetition of the fresh charges of flowers. The product thus obtained is *attar*, the fragrance of which is rich and remarkably stable. The ratio of the flower oil to the base oil determines the grade of the *attar*. For the production of cheaper grade *attar* liquid paraffin is used as a base oil in place of sandalwood oil. *Henna attar* is produced in Lucknow from *mehndi* flowers (*Lawsonia alba*). *Henna attar* produced with several other aromatic products such as vetiver, patchouli, saffron, musk, ambergris, agarwood oil etc. is highly prized in the East and Middle East countries.

Indian *attar* is, however, found to deteriorate in quality and purity and as such can hardly compete with a wide range of perfumery compounds of standard quality available in the market for perfuming hair oils, soaps, *agarbattis* etc. The demand of *attars* in the ancillary industries is on the decline on account of the supply of a wide range of perfumery compounds (mainly synthetics) of the standard quality in the market. For improving the standard of Indian products Indian Standards Institution (ISI) should codify the standard practice for making floral perfume. The total value of *attars* and allied products produced annually in India amounts to 10 crores of rupees.

Floral waters prepared from rose, *Kewda* and other flowers are used for spraying in temples and on ceremonial occasions and also for flavouring food materials. Floral waters are prepared by the distillation of flowers with water. A quantity of distillate equal to the weight of flowers charged in the still is collected; the product thus obtained is graded as "single distilled water". If it is recharged with a fresh batch of flowers and the distillate equal to the weight of the recharged flowers is obtained 'double distilled water' is prepared. And the same process is repeated for having 'triple distilled water' and so on.

There is a common practice and term to denote the grades of floral waters of rose or *Kewda*. Thus when 5 gals of perfumed water are collected by distilling 1 and 2 *mds* (*maund*) of rose flowers, the product is called *Ek mana* and *Do mana* rose water respectively. In case of *Kewda* water 1000 and 2000 flowers are used for 5 gals of distillate and known as *Ek hazara* and *Do hazara* respectively. The annual production of floral water in India is about 10,000 litres.

A time-honoured practice to prepare an Otto of rose, *Ruh Gulab*, is very simple. The rose water is placed in shallow earthenwares or metallic vessels covered with fine cloth and exposed to the cold blast of the night air in the open, a fragrant cream-like substance floats on the surface. This is collected by means of a feather in a bottle. As the day temperature rises it liquidifies to form otto.

IMPORTANT FLOWER OILS

Rose

In the history of perfumery it is recorded that the credit is given to GERONIMO ROSSI in Ravenna who discovered Otto of roses in 1574. However a legend is associated with the discovery of Otto of roses during the Mughal rule in India. A feast was arranged to celebrate the marriage of Nurjahan and Jahangir in the royal garden which had a pool filled with rose water. While walking hand in hand beside the pool the bridal couple noticed a scum-like substance floating on the surface of the water. When collected that scum was changed to oil with delicate rose perfume which was named as *attar-e-Jahangir*. Since then rose water is produced in large quantities.

Since the ancient times Rose otto or Rose oil is an important commodity of the perfumery. Until the modern method of solvent extraction was introduced rose oil was obtained mainly by adopting the process of distillation. The only advantage of distillation is to obtain a by-product—the rose water which is sometimes considered more important than the oil. Because rose water emits true rose perfume whereas distillation oil gives a different note. The reason is attributed to the loss of phenylethyl alcohol which gets dissolved in water through distillation. This active principle in its more accurate form is found in rose absolute and rose concrete obtained by means of volatile solvents. Hence the popularity of this modern method of extraction.

As far as ten centuries back rose water was first known to be distilled in Spain. In the same period it is known that Rhazes, an Arab physician, manufactured the distilled rose water. In those days the vast amount of rose water was used in medicine and perfumery in the East. The perfumery in the form of cosmetics thrived in Rome.

Jasmine

Jasmine otto is prepared from the flowers of *J. grandiflorum*. Jasmine means a rich harvest to the planters and wealth to the perfumer. The oil obtained through distillation is not good in quality. On account of this the extraction of perfume of *J. grandiflorum* by distillation is not generally adopted.

The flowers of *J. sambac* are also used for extraction of perfume. It is estimated that nearly 25000 kg of flowers are used in perfumery in India.

Tuberose

Tuberose oil, like that of jasmine, is used in high grade perfumery. Tuberose is highly suitable for extraction of perfume by enfleurage. The extraction by steam distillation is not satisfactory, because both the quality and quantity of oil produced are poor.

Kewda

Kewda attar is distilled from the mature male flowers of *Kewda*. *Kewda attar* and *Kewda* water are valued much in perfumery in India.

Orange

For orange-flower oil the process of distillation is widely used. Although various methods are tried 80 per cent of flowers are used in distillation. Once it was the principal process for producing orange-flower water rather than for the oil. Because in those days oil was looked upon as an inferior by-product. But nowadays the oil fetches very high prices.

The oil is extracted from orange-flower water by means of acetone or petroleum ether. From 3000 kilos of the water one kilo of oil is obtained. The quality of the oil thus obtained is very high.

EXTRACTION METHODS

Since time immemorial the people have been employing the method of distillation for many purposes. By simple water distillation flower oils are also extracted. The different methods which are employed in the extraction of essential oil are given below.

Distillation: Since ancient times the process of distillation has been in use for the extraction of essential oil from plant materials. In modern times, however, much improvement has been made in the construction of steam and vacuum stills, which has not only increased and cheapened the yield of oil but also has enhanced the purity of the products. The traditional still is however popular among the farmers who without any help of a factory can extract the oil from their own crop in the field. Different distillation processes are employed for separating oils from flowers. Stilled perfume is however deficient in some principles which are less volatile or decompose due to the operating temperature. The different types of distillation methods in use are water distillation, water and steam distillation, live-steam distillation, double-cooling distillation or fractional distillation and molecular or vacuum distillation.

The distillation consists of two operations: subjecting the materials to boiling water or steam and condensing vapour from the still into water and oil. The distillation apparatus, the still, consists of a retort, a condenser and a receiver. The retort is usually a copper vessel lined with tin inside. It is wider at the base than the top where a removable lid is fitted. By opening the lid the still is charged or emptied for another charge. The goose-neck of a narrow pipe that carries vapour to the condenser tube then ends to release the liquid which is collected in a glass pot. Both the operations have been greatly modified and improved in the modern technology. The first method is a time-honoured practice. It is very simple and employed usually in the field where the crop is harvested. It saves the time and labour of carrying bulk harvest to the factory site lying at a long distance. Secondly, the vegetative parts of the crop serve as cheap fuel. Thirdly, the water of rivers or irrigation canals flowing near the field is exploited to cool the condensation surface of the distillation plant. Even in absence of such water blowing breeze can serve the purpose if the condenser is drawn long to provide more surface exposed to the current of air. But the disadvantage of this process is to take extra care so that any part of the raw material (flowers) does not come in contact with hot sides of the retort and always remain covered with water during the operation. If it is not followed destructive distillation may take place which impairs the odour of the product by forming obnoxious bodies. This is, however, overcome by the process of steam distillation, in which live steam is injected into the still. The floral material is held by a perforated false bottom. Through the perforations steam passes and comes in contact with the raw material. Sometimes instead of a perforated sheet a basket hanging from the top of the still is preferred. Because it is easily removable for charging with fresh materials.

The water vapour with volatile oil passes from the still to the condensing apparatus which is cooled by means of air or water. For an air-cooling system vertical tubes are set in which vapours are condensed into water and essential oil. A water-cooled coil or Lie big condenser is universally used for having aqueous distillate which is separated into volatile oil and water. Oil being a lighter substance floats over the water and collected through an exit of a specially designed receiver. But in certain cases as in rose, *Kewda,* and orange flower oil does not get separated easily from the aqueous distillate. In such cases repeated distillation (cohobation) of the distillate is resorted to in order to cause a good amount of oil separation.

Cohobation: The aqueous distillate of many flowers like the rose, *Kewda,* orange etc. does not separate oil. Such distillate is termed 'first water'. The first water of several batches are bulked and 100 litres of the bulk is charged in an empty still and redistilled (cohobated) very slowly. Until 10 litres of the distillate is collected, which is known as 'second water'. The remaining 90 litres of the first water of the still is used in the fresh charge with flowers. The second water is apt to separate oil. Hence it is collected in glass bottles and allowed to stand for several hours after which oil is found to float over the water, which is collected by means of decantation.

Another type of water of steam distillation at a reduced atmospheric pressure is also recommended for the production of much superior quality of oil with fine odour and without any burnt off note. The principle is closely related to modern molecular distillation by which very delicate organic chemicals like vitamins which cannot be heated to their normal boiling points are extracted. For reducing pressures the apparatus must be very solid and air tight involving a high cost. The high price of the oil might be justified for its true-to-note perfume of volatile nature.

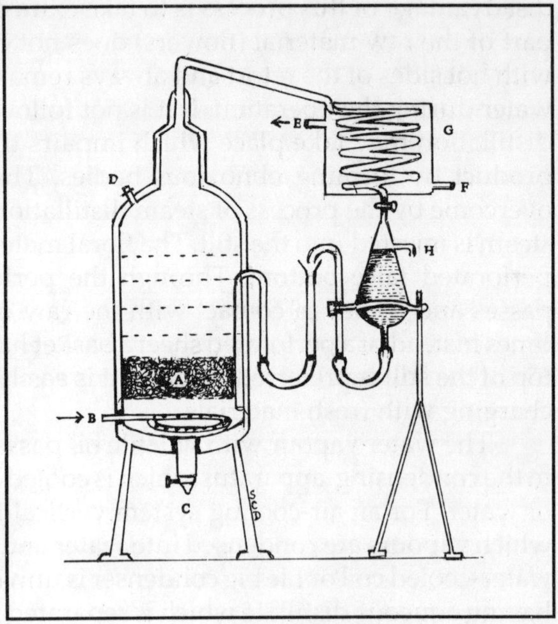

A STILL FOR AUTOMATIC COHOBATION
A. Charge (Flower) B. Steam Inlet
C. Drain D. Safety Valve
E. Water Outlet F. Water Inlet
G. Condenser H. Oil Outlet

In case of some flowers such as the rose, *Kewda* etc. the separation of oil from the perfumed water is a difficult task.

To get rid of the difficulty the process of fractional distillation as applied for the separation of the different ingredients from the crude petroleum oil has to be applied. On applying this principle the National Botanical Research Institute of Lucknow has designed and patented (Indian Patent No. 130396) an apparatus. This new apparatus is so constructed as to make the separation of oil and the collection of the perfumed water automatic. The author also has developed a more simple apparatus in which the concentration of volatile oil vapour is immensely increased in the fractional column which on concentration is automatically separated from the aqueous distillate. A temperature gradient is formed in the vertical fractional column, which tends to condense the water which is less volatile. Hence the vapour that passes to the condenser is concentrated with more volatile substance, the essential oil.

Enfleurage: The great advantage of this process is to obtain true-to-note perfume. Because in most cases the quality of perfume is deteriorated by heating process of distillation.

In this process of enfleurage cold fat is employed to absorb volatile perfume oil which is then extracted from the fat treated with alcohol. The refined lard or deodorised hydrogenated oil is spread thinly over the both sides of a glass plate fitted in the middle of a wooden frame so that each side of the plate becomes a tray to hold flowers. A number of trays are stacked one above another with fresh flowers sandwiched between the two plates so that volatile perfume cannot escape but absorbed into the fat. In order to increase the absorbing surface the layer of fat is combed to form furrows. The stale flowers are replaced with fresh flowers every day until the fat is saturated with perfume.

The pomade (perfume saturated fat) is scraped from the plates and treated with 95 per cent alcohol. The extract is cooled to 10-15°C and filtered. The clean filtrate thus obtained is known as 'extrait' which is used straightway in perfumery. In order to obtain the absolute of enfleurage the solvent (alcohol) should be removed by vacuum distillation.

A unique method of enfleurage is adopted to prepare hair oil (*Gulroghan*) from the flower of jasmine (*Bela* or *Chameli*), *Kewda* and *henna* in Kanauj, Jaunpur, Ghazipur and Sikandarpur in U.P. The process is as follows.

Clean and husked sesame seeds are made to absorb perfume from flowers arranged in alternate layers of flowers and seeds; then the seeds are pressed to collect perfumed oil.

Seeds are spread in a thin layer on clean ground open to fresh air. A layer of flowers is laid on it. And other similar layers of flowers and of seeds are superimposed to a stack of a few feet high. The exhausted flowers are removed after 24 hours and fresh flowers are charged. The process is repeated for a week or so until the seeds are saturated with perfume. The seeds thus enfleuraged are pressed to yield fragrant oil which is considered an excellent hair oil. It is also used as an ingredient of compounded *attars*.

Another method of enfleurage which permits the use of oil instead of fat is practised on a cottage scale. A stock of fresh flowers is covered with a silken cloth smeared with olive oil or sandalwood oil which is finely spread over it. The flowers are charged with a fresh lot every day. But in case of tuberose, flowers are replaced at alternate days. When the oil absorbed in the cloth is saturated with perfume the cloth is squeezed to separate the perfumed oil.

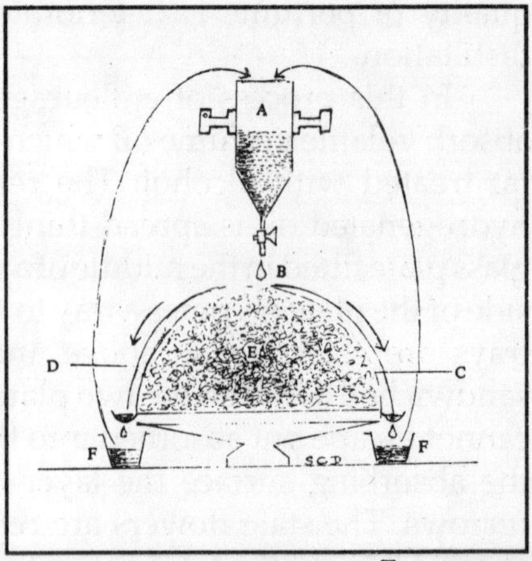

ENFLEURAGE
VERTICAL SECTION OF AN APPARATUS
DEVISED BY THE AUTHOR
A. Oil can B. Drop of oil
C. Perforated plastic basket
D. Silk cloth covering the basket
E. Fragrant Flowers
F. Glass cup holding dripping oil

A very useful apparatus has been developed by the author which makes the process very simple. Because spraying and squeezing operations have been eliminated in this process. The oil is stored in a overhead oil pot from which oil drips over a canopy of cloth covering a basket containing flowers. The base of the cloth ends in a pot which collects the perfumed oil that passes downwards through the cloth. The oil collected in the bottom pot is lifted to the top pot once a day. Every day the flowers of the basket are replaced with fresh ones. The process is repeated until the oil is saturated with perfume. In spite of the modern processes of extraction namely 'solvent extraction', 'fractional distillation', 'molecular distillation' etc. the enfleurage methods which were introduced in the beginning of the perfumery are still popular. In the Grasse region of Southern France and in the northern part of India the enfleurage processes of extraction were employed first in perfumery. In the hands of the French perfumers the expertise gradually developed to make it a viable process even in the midst of the tremendous development of chemical technology during the second half of the present century.

Another simple method of enfleurage is to pass the perfumed air through a deodorised oil contained in a series of wolf bottles by a very small suction pump (shown in the diagram). The perfumed oil thus obtained can be directly marketed as perfumed hair oil.

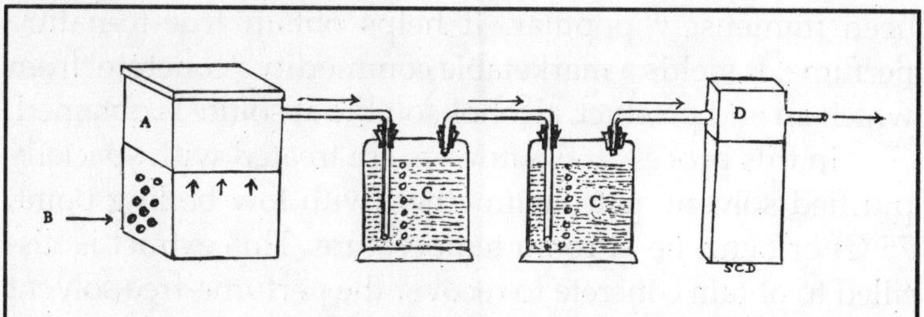

MODIFIED ENFLEURAGE

A. Box (with perforated bottom) containing Fresh Flowers

B. Air Passage Holes

C. Bottle containing oil (arrow marks indicating air passage)

D. Small Suction Pump

Maceration: The process of maceration involves the extraction by hot fat quite opposite to the enfleurage in which cold fat is employed. In maceration hot oil enters the tissue of flowers thus coming in contact of perfume. This process was introduced in the earliest days of perfumery when the modern methods were quite unknown. A batch of fat heated to 80°C and a charge of flowers is treated at that temperature for 30 minutes after which the fat is allowed to cool down gradually at the room temperature. Normally it will take an hour during which it continues macerating the flowers. Then the mass is reheated to melt that facilitates separation of the exhausted flowers by sieving. It is however not easy to recover the adhering fat from the exhausted flowers. Hydraulic presses or centrifuges are generally employed to recover the fat. Usually 10 charges are required to saturate the fat with perfume. A single batch of charge should be the one-fourth of the fat in weight.

To obtain perfume from the fat the same process has to be followed as with the pomade of enfleurage. In India, however, the macerated oil is directly marketed as hair oil. In that case deodorised oils of sesame, cocoanut etc. are used instead of tallow or lard.

Solvent extraction: The extraction of flower perfume with volatile solvent is obviously a modern process which has been immensely popular. It helps obtain true-to-nature perfume. It yields a marketable commodity, 'concrete' from which an end product, alcohol-soluble absolute is obtained.

In this process fresh flowers are treated with specially purified solvent, petroleum ether (with low boiling point, 75°C) or benzene at room temperature. This extract is distilled to obtain concrete to recover the perfume-free solvent for reuse.

To treat the flowers with solvent a rotary extractor is used. It consists of a tin-lined iron drum rotating on a horizontal axis. For holding flowers into separate chambers the drum is divided into four compartments with perforated metal partitions. The extractor is charged with flowers and the solvent is poured in at the rate of 2 litre/kg of flowers. After closing the lid the extractor is rotated slowly for ten minutes. In this way the solvent will absorb the perfume of the flowers.

In order to derive more perfume each batch of flowers is treated thrice with the solvent and conversely each lot of solvent is treated three times. The final extract is distilled to recover the solvent for reuse. This distillation has its two phases: the recovery of three-fourth solvent is done in the normal pressure and the rest is recovered in a vacuum still. In the first phase the extract is drawn to the evaporator which is heated at 75°-80°C over a water bath or steam jacket. The temperature of the evaporator should carefully be maintained by a thermostatic control so that the control will switch off as soon as it reaches 80°C. In this process the solvent is first drawn into the evaporator and then the current is switched on. The solvent vapour is passed through the condenser cooled by circulating water. The process will continue until three-fourths of the solvent is condensed for reuse. The remaining one-fourth is taken to a vacuum still for complete recovery. After the complete evaporation of the solvent a semi-solid wax-like brown substance is left in the still, which is 'concrete'. Although concrete is a marketable commodity further processing is required to obtain 'absolute' from it.

The concrete has to be purified in order to separate essence, wax and colouring matters. The concrete is taken in a glass or stainless steel container for grinding with alcohol. A pastel with mortar is also used with advantage. Warm absolute alcohol is poured into the pastel containing concrete. After grinding for some time perfume gets dissolved in the alcohol which is filtered under vacuum. The residue still contains a good amount of perfume. One kilo of concrete requires 4 litres of alcohol to be treated.

The treated alcohol is filtered. The filtrate is concentrated slowly at a low temperature in a vacuum still. The alcohol vapour is condensed into liquid alcohol which is used again after recovery. After complete evaporation of alcohol a viscous brown oil-like substance is left in the still, which is known as 'absolute'. The yield of absolute may be 40%-60% of the concrete.

Solvent: The commercial food-grade hexane has been found suitable for extraction of floral concrete and as such is used for this purpose throughout the world. Before using it should be purified with liquid paraffin (white oil). For this purpose it is treated with liquid paraffin and distilled at 70°C. The residue obtained is rejected as impurities. The purified hexane is a colourless liquid with a boiling point ranging from 60° to 80°C.

For perfume extraction and recovery of solvent for recycling Tamil Nadu Agricultural University (Coimbatore-3) has designed a pilot plant which is marketed by LCT Industries (Trichy Road, Coimbatore-18). It has essential four parts—extractor, evaporator, condenser and vacuum distillation unit.

OIL EXTRACTION OF IMPORTANT FLOWERS

Rose

Now over 13000 kilos of rose otto are produced annually in few countries of the world, namely, Bulgaria, Turkey, India and Morocco from the flowers of *Rosa centifolia* and *Rosa damascena*. The largest producer being Bulgaria where four types of extraction are in practice. These are by open fire with small retorts placed mainly in the farmer's field, open fire with large retorts, modern steam stills and the extraction of oils by volatile solvents.

Gradually, however, the small distillers do not find their enterprise much paying due to the impact of the modern technology employed in the large establishments. Most small growers now harvest and send their roses to the large distilleries or solvent extraction centres.

The attempts have been made to represent accurate rose scent by the use of synthetic materials. But the process is far from satisfactory. The use of rose otto is however prohibitive in cheap and ordinary perfumes, soaps and cosmetics on account of its high prices.

India was once renowned for the manufacture of perfumes. Now both rose water and rose *attar* are produced in old methods. The beautiful rose fields that sweeten the air are found around Ghazipur in Uttar Pradesh. A hair oil 'Gulroghan' is produced from sesame seeds treated to absorb perfume from rose petals (see Enfleurage). Much of the rose otto produced in other countries is sent to Southern France where at Grasse the perfumery industry has flourished.

Harvesting and Storage: The flowers are picked immediately after opening in the early morning. In handling and storing care should be taken so that the delicate petals are not bruised. They should not be wasted between the operations—collection and distillation. To achieve this end the distillation unit has to be placed near the field. If the distillation is delayed due to the large quantity of produce the flowers should be stored in cold water contained in cemented cisterns. In order to check the evaporation of volatile oil 5% brine water may be used in the cisterns.

In the different growing centres of Uttar Pradesh Rose water is distilled in the conventional method with direct fired stills. Water is poured into the still at the rate of 20-25 litres for every 10 kg of flowers. The distillation period is usually 4-5 hours. This process however cannot separate Rose oil (Otto of Rose) from rose water.

As the aqueous distillation of rose does not separate oil such distillation is termed as 'first water'. The first water of several batches are bulked and 100 litres of the bulk is charged in empty still and redistilled (cohobated) very slowly until 10 litres of the distillate is collected, which is known as 'second water'. The remaining 90 litres of the first water of the still is used in fresh charge with flowers. The second water is apt to separate oil. Hence it is collected in glass bottles and allowed to stand for several hours, after which oil is found to float over water, which is collected by means of decantation.

Rose Water: Rose water is one of the floral waters used for spraying in temples and on ceremonial occasions, and also for flavouring food materials. Rose waters are prepared by the distillation of flowers with water. A quantity of distillate equal to the weight of the flowers charged in the still is collected, the product thus obtained is graded as 'single distilled water'. If the single distilled water is recharged with a fresh batch of flowers and the distillate equal to the weight of recharged flowers is obtained the 'double distilled water' is prepared. And the same process is repeated for having 'triple distilled water' and so on.

There is a common practice and terms to denote the grades of floral water of rose. Thus when 5 gals of perfumed water are collected by distilling 1 and 2 *mds* of rose flowers the product is called *Ek mana* and *Do mana* rose water respectively. The annual production of floral waters in India is about 10,000 litres.

Otto of Rose: A time-honoured practice to prepare an otto of rose, Ruh Gulab, is very simple. The rose water is placed in shallow earthenwares or metallic vessels covered with a fine cloth and exposed to the cold blast of the night air in the open. A scented cream-like substance floats on the surface. This is collected by means of a feather in a bottle. As the day temperature rises it liquidifies. But the disadvantage of this process is to take extra care so that any part of the raw material does not come in contact with the hot sides of the still and always remain covered with water during the operation. If it is not followed destructive distillation may take place which impairs the odour of the product by forming obnoxious bodies.

This is however overcome by the process of steam distillation, in which live steam is injected into the still. The floral material is held by a perforated false bottom. Through the perforations steam passes and comes in contact with the raw material.

Rose oil does not get separated easily from the aqueous

distillate. Repeated distillation (cohobation) of the distillate is cumbersome. To get rid of the difficulty a modern still has been designed in which the cohobation process is automatic. The automatic return of distillation water to the still causes the rising vapour to contain more oil which floats on the distillate on condensation.

In Bulgaria the Damask rose is grown in the 'Famous Valley of Roses' which is situated 200 km off from Sophia eastwards. The area under cultivation is 1000 sq kilometres. It is divided into ten districts of which Kazenlik being the main. Around 2 lakhs of people of 150 villages of the valley are engaged in rose growing and perfumery industry.

Some million kilos of rose flowers are produced there. The most productive area being at an altitude of 300-700 metres. *Rosa damascena* constitutes 90 per cent of the rose population. One kilo of flowers counts 750 blooms. 3500 kilos of blooms yield one kilo of rose otto. For a drop of oil you need 170 blooms of *R. damascena*.

Moroccan rose otto has a good market. Roses are grown there in Dades Valley lying 300 km southeast of Atlas range. One important place is Marakesh at an altitude of 3000-5000 ft and very close to Sahara (desert).

The quantity of flowers grown is around 2000 tons. Both distillation and solvent extraction methods are employed. The production of oil is variable, because 3000-5000 kilo produce 1 kg of oil. The annual production is around 450 kilo of otto and 3000 kilo of concrete. Moroccan oil is not as good as that of Bulgaria. It is cheap; hence popular.

In Anatolia (Turkey) the species *R. damascena* is grown at an altitude of 3000 ft. There is a Rose Co-operative in Isparta. The annual production being 25 kg of rose otto and 250 kg of rose concrete. The farmers of Grasse (France) have set up distillery units producing an excellent oil.

The production in France is very low in comparison with Bulgaria. The processes of maceration (20%), solvent extraction (70%) and distillation (10%) are employed. The species used is *R. centifolia* which is grown 10,000 bushes per hectare. The yield varies from 2000-5000 kilos of flowers per hectare.

Italy also grows *R. centifolia*. There 6000-10,000 kilos of flowers yield 1 kilo of rose otto. In 1968 a survey was made to assess the yield of rose flowers and its products in the different countries which is as follows:

	(Flowers in tons)
Bulgaria	5000
USSR	5000
Morocco	2500
Turkey	2000
France	300

Bulgaria produces 1 kilo of oil from 3500 kilos of flowers
Anatolia produces 1 kilo of oil from 4000 kilos of flowers
Morocco produces 1 kilo of oil from 350 kilos of flowers
France produces 1 kilo of oil from 12000 kilos of flowers

(In France the rose water is the main product and oil is a by-product.)

Jasmine

Flowers of *J. grandiflorum* open in the evening from 5-7 P.M. Fully open flowers should be picked early in the morning. Most of the volatile-perfume oil is lost if the flowers are not picked and used before 8 A.M. Jasmine flowers continue to emit perfume even long after picking from the plant. Hence the flowers are highly suitable for enfleurage. The oil obtained through distillation is not good in quality. On account of this the extraction of perfume of *J. grandiflorum* by distillation is not generally adopted. Damaged, bruised or chopped flowers should not be used for solvent extraction. Because such flowers yield concrete with more percentage of unwanted wax and other substances. The solvent extraction is more a modern method. Nowadays it is employed in most parts of the world. The yield of concrete varies between 0.28 to 0.3% w/w. Although the concrete is marketable product, jasmine concrete is not used in perfumery. Its perfumery ingredients are further purified by extraction with 95% alcohol, and thus jasmine absolute is obtained. A ton of fresh jasmine flowers yield 2.8 to 3 kg of concrete which in turn on alcoholic extraction gives 1.3 to 1.5 kg of absolute (otto) depending upon the age of the plantation, season and time of collection and extraction of flowers including the efficiency of processing unit. The concrete on treatment with superheated steam between 88°C and 92°C at 35 to 40 mm pressure gives 10.6-23.5% of volatile oil. The volatile oil in this method is not produced industrially, but the method is used only for testing the quality of a particular concrete.

Jasmine concrete is a reddish brown waxy mass with an odour of jasmine flowers. It is partly soluble in 95% alcohol. The absolute on the other hand is viscous, clear, yellowish brown liquid possessing delicate odour of fresh jasmine flowers.

Jasmine concrete and absolute are two amongst those natural perfumery materials which possess unique odoriferous characteristics not yet imitated by the synthetic process or compounding isolates from natural essential oils. Jasmine means a rich harvest to the planters and wealth to the perfumer.

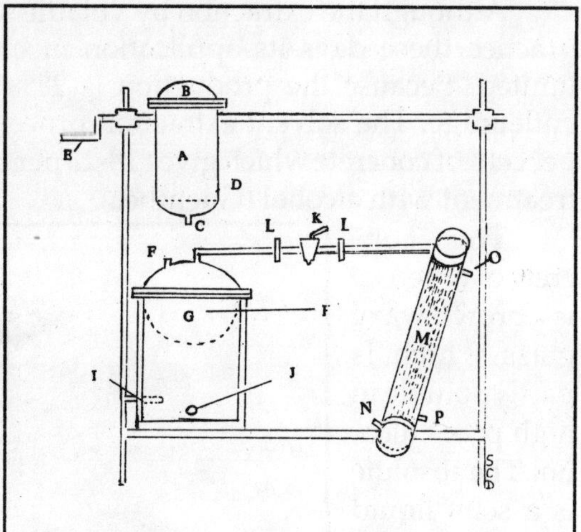

JASMINE OIL EXTRACTION PLANT
(Designed by T.N. Agricultural University Coimbatore)
A. Mixing Chamber B. Lid C. Drain Cock D. Filter E. Handle F. Inlet for Solvent G. Bowl (Distillation) H. Evaporator I. Thermostat J. Immersion Heater K. Valve (Regulator) L. Flange M. Condenser N. Inlet (Cooling Water) O. Outlet (Hot Water) P. Recovery Port

Yield of Concrete: Amongst the varieties of *J. auriculatum* 'Short Round' recorded the highest percentage of concrete yield. But in the total yield per hectare the variety 'Co1' recorded the highest with 28.23 kg. In *J. grandiflorum* cv 'Co1' (Pitchi) recorded the highest concrete yield of 29.42 kg which was closely followed by the cv 'Thimmapuram' with 27.14 kg per hectare.

Tuberose

Tuberose oil, like that of jasmine, is used in high grade perfumery. Tuberose is highly suitable for extraction of perfume by enfleurage as the flowers continue to produce perfume for 48 hours after opening. The absolute is extracted from the pomade of enfleurage with alcohol. 150 kilos of flowers produce about 1 kilo of absolute.

Although the extraction by volatile solvents is in wide practice these days its application in case of tuberose is limited. Because the production is 28% less than that of enfleurage. The solvent extraction process yields 0.08-0.11 per cent of concrete which gives 18-23 per cent of absolute on treatment with alcohol (Guenther).

The concrete of tuberose is a brown waxy mass which is partly soluble in high proof alcohol. The absolute is a semi-liquid brownish mass with powerful and lasting odour, truly suggestive of that emitted by fresh flowers. This most expensive floral product is

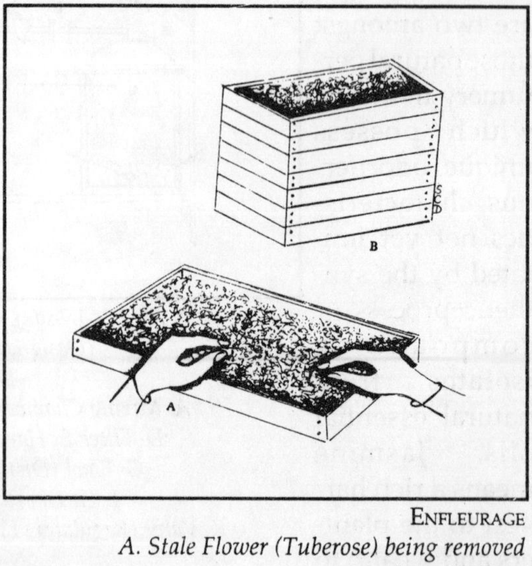

ENFLEURAGE
A. Stale Flower (Tuberose) being removed from the Tray
B. Stack of Trays charged with Flowers

used only in high grade perfumes.

Extraction by steam distillation is not satisfactory, because both the quality and quantity of oil produced are poor.

Tuberose oil contains geraniol, nerol, farnesol, benzyl alcohol etc.

Kewda

In this country *Kewda* oil is obtained through distillation in the district of Ganjam in Orissa. The chief centres of distillation are as follows:

Indrakhi (15 km from Berhampur, Ganjam)
Tulu (13 km from Berhampur, Ganjam)
Kevapalli (12 km from Berhampur, Ganjam)
Agraham (8 km from Berhampur, Ganjam)

All these villages are very near to the sea (Bay of Bengal). About more than sixty distilleries are there around these areas where *Kewda* bushes grow abundantly. It is estimated that about four lakhs of *Kewda* bushes grow in the district of Ganjam, which produce two crores of flowers annually.

The chief centres of *Kewda* flowers are Chhatrapur, Ganjam village, Gopalpur, Jagannathpur, Kanisi, Indrakhi, Tulu, Kevapalli, Agraham and all the nearby villages in between Chhatrapur and Ganjam village.

Kewda flowers are collected from the plants during early morning, at about 5 A.M. They are brought to the distilleries. Although the distilleries are owned by the local people (one of the owners is P.S.N. Reddy of Indrakhi) the merchants of essential oil from Kanauj, Ajmer, Lucknow etc. come to these places for the production of *Kewda* oil. According to their requirements different grades of *Kewda* oil and water are produced. There is one *Kewda* Flowers Association in this village to improve the condition of the *Kewda* villages and to look after the interest of the *Kewda* flower growers.

Distillation: The following ingredients are used for the distillation:

(i) *Kewda* flowers
(ii) Sandalwood oil
(iii) Other base oils
(iv) Liquid paraffin
(v) Water
(vi) Firewood

Distillation plant: A big copper vessel of 300-400 litre capacity is used as retort having tightly fitted lid. A vapour tube of bamboo, one end of which is fitted to the lid of the

KEWDA DISTILLATION
A. Big Copper Vessel (Retort) B. Fire by burning Firewood C. Cap D. A Condenser of Bamboo Tube wrapped with Hessian Cloth E. Small Copper Vessel (Receiver) F. Water for cooling the Receiver G. Tap for taking out Kewda Water

retort and other to a small copper pot held in a pool of cold water, is used with advantage. The retort is fitted to a fire place for heating. Usually 6-8 plants are erected in series.

The retort is charged with 80 litres of water and 700-800 flowers by opening the lid. Then the lid is replaced and made air tight applying mud. The fire is kindled with firewood. In the beginning 5 kg of sandalwood oil is taken in the small copper vessel. Water vapour with volatile oil passes through the bamboo tube and gets condensed in the small copper pot held in a pool of cold water. The *Kewda* oil mixed with the aqueous distillate amounts to 5 kg, then the second vessel with 5 kg of base oil (other than sandalwood oil) is filled and kept until 7-8 kg of distillate is deposited. Then a third vessel with another type of base oil is used till 10-12 kg of *Kewda* water is obtained. Thus three grades of *Kewda attar* are produced. But for a good concentration of *Kewda* oil in the *attar* the process is repeated with the fresh charge of flowers. Next day the base oil is treated with vapours of successive charges of 20-25 thousand *Kewda* flowers. At the end of each charge *Kewda* water (aqueous distillate) is taken out through the plugged hole of the vessels. The production season lasts for two months i.e. from the middle of June to the middle of August.

Kewda attar and *Kewda* water have different uses. *Kewda attar* is very popular in Indian perfumery, which finds its extensive use in cosmetics, soaps, hair oils, tobacco flavouring, *Agarbatti* and in various scents and bouquets. For favouring foods, drinks, sweets and confectioneries *Kewda attar* and *Kewda* water are in common use. They are more popular in North India where the people have a special liking for them on the festive occasions.

Amongst other methods of extraction the process of enfleurage is also adopted. In this way volatile oil is absorbed by sesame seeds (see Enfleurage). The oil then extracted from the sesame seeds is used as perfumed hair oil. In the coastal districts of West Bengal and Orissa commercial catechu is flavoured with *Kewda* perfume by the rural folk (see 'Recipe').

The experiments for extraction with volatile solvents have been successful. The oil obtained possesses strong fascinating odour. The rate of yield being 0.1-0.3 per cent. The H.B. Technological Institute of Kanpur has developed a peculiar process of extraction, which is the amalgamation of distillation and solvent extraction methods. The advantage of this new method is yet to be known.

Orange

Distillation has always been employed for extraction of orange blossom oil as it yields much more than the other processes including volatile solvents. The average yield being 900-1100 grams from 1000 kg of flowers. The yield of oil recorded in the south of France is 1500 grams from 1000 kg of flowers. In Tunis oil of neroli is produced by distillation which can compete well with the French product. In Charabot and Lonone it has been found by experiments that dry flowers yield a higher percentage of oil than the fresh. Flowers collected in a fine weather of spring yield better than those of rainy season. Previously orange flower-water was considered as a significant by-product. But today it is much esteemed in commerce for its delightful fragrance of fresh blossoms. In perfumery of today Neroli oil is considered a powerful ingredient.

The aqueous distillate from distillation plant may be subjected to solvent extraction. In this novel process flower-water is treated with volatile solvent like acetone, petroleum ether to extract the perfume. The product is very powerful, its odour is about ten times stronger than the normal oil.

The different grades of orange flower-water are sold in the perfumery market. Their gradation depends on oil-content of the flower. Generally distillates are classified on this basis. The first part consisting of the four-fifths of the total water used contains more oil than the remaining one-fifth. The oil content of the first part has been found to be 0.031 per cent whereas the last part contains 0.008 per cent only. The cohobated water however contains much more oil (see Cohobation).

Champaka (*M. champaca*)

Champaka oil can be extracted from the flowers of *M. champaca*, *M. alba* (*M. longifolia*). In India it is distilled from *Swarna champa* (*M. champaca*) and obtained as *Champaka attar* in Paralakhemundi (120 km from Berhampur in the south) in the district of Ganjam. Outside of India the flowers of the species *longifolia* are used in Philippines and Java for oil extraction. In Java both yellow (*M. champaca*) and white (*M. longifolia*) flowers are mixed for distillation.

The so called *Champaka* oil of commerce is however chiefly produced from a mixture of various other flowers and isolates.

Solvent extraction process with petroleum ether is employed in Reunion Island and Madagascar. The yield of concrete varies from 0.13-0.20 per cent.

The absolute (otto) obtained from the concrete is just the half of its weight. The absolute has a very fine odour closely approximating the live flowers. Very small quantities of oil, say about 5-10 kg per year, are produced by the solvent extraction process. *Champaka* otto is an exquisite ingredient of enchanting creations of French perfumery.

Magnolia (*M. grandiflora*)

Magnolia flowers well in humid and hilly regions. Spring and summer being the suitable period of flowering. Though highly fragrant it is not found to be sold as cut flower.

Essential oil has been extracted experimentally from *Magnolia grandiflora*. But there is no information if the flower is used in commercial oil extraction.

Maulsarai (*Mimusops elengi*)

Maulsarai, like nyctanthes, showers its flowers (caducous corollas) before daybreak. They are valued much for garlands which are used for adorning lady's hair. They emit perfume even after drying.

Flowers are distilled for perfume. Fresh flowers on water distillation yield 0.01% essential oil. But no commercial production of oil has been reported.

Kamini (*Murraya paniculata*)

A flowering twig of murraya looks like a bouquet which is collected in the evening for vase decoration and sweet perfume.

Both flowers and leaves contain essential oil. Leaves

yield 0.01% volatile oil (dark coloured) on steam distillation. Flowers are reported to be used in Java for making cosmetics.

Mehndi (*L. inermis*)

The essential oil of *Lawsonia* is known as '*Henna* oil'. It has been used in perfumery since a long time. In this country it is commercially extracted in Lucknow and Banaras. The process of steam distillation is employed, which yields 0.01-0.02% of an essential oil with brown or dark brown colour and a strong aroma reminiscent of tea rose and mignonette. Hence its name 'Jamaica mignonette' in the West Indies.

Uses of Leaves: The pigment extracted from the leaves of *Lawsonia* is known as 'Henna'. It is orange in colour and has long been used for colouring hands and palms, soles of feet and finger nails. It is also used for dyeing hair. The tails and manes of animals are sometimes dyed with *henna*. It has also its uses in colouring leathers and skins. The dyeing properties of *henna* are due to the presence of *Lawsone* (2-hydroxyl, 4-naphthaquinone).

In order to bring about desired colours and shades *henna* is compounded with other dyes obtained from either plant materials or chemicals. For example, a mixture of 1 part of *henna* and two parts of indigo imparts a brown tint; while 1 part of *henna*, 3 parts of indigo gives a dark brown colour.

The acreage under *henna* cultivation in India is not available. The annual production of dried leaves is known to vary from 25,000-30,000 kg. The major producer is Punjab followed by Gujarat, Madhya Pradesh and Rajasthan (Brochure on Marketing Henna 1955). *Henna* is marketed in form of powder and the principal marketing centre is Faridabad.

A decoction of *henna* has recently come very much into vogue in shampoos, brilliantines, etc. and is extremely used for dyeing hair.

Nyctanthes (*N. arbor-tristis*)

Nyctanthes belongs to the same family as jasmine. So flowers contain an essential oil like that of jasmine. The water distillation method is employed for the separation of oil. The solvent extraction process with benzene has also been tried with success. The yield from water distillation is 0.0045 per cent. The concrete obtained by solvent extraction is 0.055% which on steam distillation yields 10.5% of otto.

Though the quantity of oil obtained by water distillation is very low in comparison with that of solvent extraction the process justifies its utility for the low cost of production and collection of flowers. Distillation by the simple pot-distillation process may be taken up as a cottage industry. The product will find a good market in rural areas. Rural soap factories and cheap cosmetic industries will be able to use natural oil cheaply instead of high priced synthetics manufactured in the big industrial cities. This will immensely increase the prospect of rural employment and consequently the rural development. Enfleurage and maceration processes are also very useful for small and home units.

The bright orange corolla tubes of the flowers contain a colouring matter—'*nyctanthin*' which is used for colouring silk and cotton. It imparts a very beautiful orange or golden colour. As the colour is not permanent certain chemicals are used to make it stable. The decoction is prepared from corolla tubes, and fabrics are steeped in it for dyeing. Lime juice and alum added to the dye bath render the colour more stable.

Plumeria

The flowers of plumerias have a use in making perfumes. It is obvious that the flowers of strongly scented varieties are used. They emit perfume for a long time even after picking. Hence the enfleurage of fresh flowers gives the best result. The steam distillation of fresh flowers yields 0.04-0.07 per cent of essential oil. The plumeria oil is known to possess an antifungal property.

Sambac (*J. sambac*)

The flowers of sambac are also used for extraction of perfume. It is estimated that nearly 25000 kg of flowers are used in perfumery in India. The extraction of perfume with petroleum ether yields 0.48% of concrete which may produce 26.39% of absolute. It is deep red in colour. Sambac otto possesses a very pleasing and lasting note and can be used in the preparation of high grade perfume and cosmetics.

Juhi (*J. auriculatum*)

In this country *Juhi* flowers are used for making perfumed oil and *attars*. The method of operation is same as employed for *J. grandiflorum*. The otto produced experimentally at Kanpur has a dark red colour and pleasant and delightful fragrance of fresh flowers.

RECIPES

The following recipes are prepared directly from the petals of fragrant flowers. They are, however, produced on the cottage scale. No industry of small, medium or large scale is known to manufacture these recipes.

Gulkand: Sugar and rose petals in equal proportions are pounded to prepare a conserve which is considered a good tonic to brace up health. In this country the petals of the Damask rose or Edward rose are used for this purpose.

Pankhuri: Dried rose petals of fragrant varieties are used to prepare cold drinks. In certain places of the country it is a favourite drink in summer months. Dried petals are known as *Pankhuri*.

Gul-Roghan (Hair oil): It is prepared by the process of enfleurage or maceration using sesame seeds (*til*) and fragrant flowers or boiling oil with fragrant flowers (see Extraction Methods).

Pot-Pouri: It is prepared from the dry petals of scented flowers, orris root, cinnamon, cloves, nutmeg and rind of orange.

The petals should be dried in shade. Orris root, cinnamon, cloves and nutmeg should be ground and orange peels chopped before use.

All the ingredients are mixed and ground to prepare the conserve. To increase its flavour few drops of any suitable essential oil may be added. The product must be kept dry or mould will develop. For this reason it is prepared in winter when the weather is sufficiently dry.

Scented Catechu: Catechu used with *pan* (betel leaf with areca nut) is flavoured with the oil of scented flowers. *Kewda* scent is favoured most.

In the villages of coastal regions catechu is flavoured with *Kewda* flowers by the process of enfleurage. The catechu is moistened to mould into a flat. A number of flats are arranged one above another between the layers of *Kewda* spathes. Follow the process as described in 'Enfleurage'. After a week or so the whole mass of catechu will absorb perfume and get scented. The perfumed catechu thus prepared is preserved and marketed, which has a great demand in the *pan* stalls. *Kewda* water is also used to prepare liquid catechu for using in *pans*.

Appendix

A. Glossary (General)

Absolute	Pure otto obtained by solvent extraction process.
Adventitious root	See glossary of Chapter 1.
Agarbatti	Incense stick.
Agarwood oil	Essential oil extracted from Agarwood (*Aquilaria agalocha*). It is also known as 'Aguru' in Sanskrit.
Anthesis	See glossary of Chapter 1.
Aqueous distillate	Condensed water and oil.
Attar	Perfume in fixation oil.
Bare root	Plants with open roots (without soil).
Base oil	Oil used to absorb perfume oil from distillate.
Braille	Printing with embossed letters for the blind.
Carpel	See glossary of Chapter 1.
Corolla tube	See glossary of Chapter 1.
Concrete	A substance containing wax, perfume and colouring matter. It is an intermediate product of solvent extraction.
Damask scent	Sweet perfume of the Damask rose.
Destructive distillation	Deterioration of distillate by overheating.
Eau-de-cologne	Perfumed toilet water.
Etiolation	Describing condition of a plant part devoid of chlorophyll due to the non-exposure to sunlight.

Extrait	Alcoholic washings of perfumed fat (Pomade).
Fine rose	The rose (spout) of a water can with fine perforations.
Flower water	Perfumed water obtained as a distillate, e.g. 'Rose water', '*Kewda* water' etc.
Fractional distillation	Substances having boiling points of minimum difference are separated by this process. Kerosene, petrol, diesel etc. are separated from the crude oil by fractional distillation.
Gamma ray	A radioactive ray which has application in mutation breeding.
Hybrid tea scent	A mixture of scents of tea roses and other roses.
Ikebana	Flower arranging after Japanese style.
In situ	In the permanent situation.
Laterite soil	Red soil of tropical region. It has a use in making roads.
Leafmould	Decomposed leaves forming humus.
Liquid paraffin	White oil, a petroleum product.
Loam	A soil formed by a mixture of clay and sand in equal proportions.
Microbe	Micro-organism which can be seen under a microscope. It causes disease, fermentation, or other useful or harmful changes in organic bodies.
Molecular distillation	Distillation in low temperature under vacuum.
Mono type	Reference to a genus/species composed of a single type.
Mulch	A protective covering of straw,

	leaves or coarse manure spread over the root zone of plants to retain moisture, kill weeds etc.
Mutation breeding	Induced breeding caused by radioactive rays or strong chemicals.
Narcissus	A bulbous plant of the family *Amaryllidaceae*. It is associated with a Greek legend.
Plant Patent Act	An Act in favour of the interest of a plant breeder. Under this Act a cultivar originated by a breeder can be multiplied for a commercial purpose by its originator alone.
Pomade	Tallow saturated with perfume in the process of enfleurage.
Pre-cooling	A process of subjecting perishables like flowers and vegetables to a temperature just above the freezing point before sending to the market.
Retort	A vessel with a long narrow neck turned downwards, used for distilling liquids.
Secateurs	Clippers used for pruning bushes.
Soil	The upper layer of the earth in which plants grow. It is formed by a series of changes in presence of sun and shower, air, microbial activities and plant residues through ages. Its depth hardly exceeds 25 cm.
Solvent	A volatile chemical for absorbing perfume in the solvent extraction process.
Spathes	See glossary of Chapter 1.

Sport	A product of a sudden heritable variation, spontaneous or artificial in the character of the plant part. Sporting is also known as 'mutation'.
Stamens	See glossary of Chapter 1.
Steam distillation	Distillation by heating the charge with steam instead of boiling water.
Stilt root	See glossary of Chapter 1.
Sun baking	Forming a crusted layer by sun and air.
Tea rose	A class of rose having tea scent.
Temperature gradient	A slope made by gradual rise or fall of temperature.
Vacuum distillation	Distillation in absence of atmospheric pressure.
Vacuum Still	A distillation plant for distilling in absence of atmospheric pressure.
Vase life	Life of a cut flower in the vase.
Volatile oil	Essèntial oil which vaporises quickly.
Woodash	Ash obtained on burning wood which is grey or white in colour.

B. Select Cultivars

J. grandiflorum	'Co1', 'Pichi', Thimmapuram', 'Coimbatore', 'Lucknow' & 'Pink Pin'
J. officinale	'Affine' (originated in Shibpur Botanical Gardens, Howrah)
J. auriculatum	'Co1', 'Mullai', 'Parimullai', 'Large Round', 'Short Point' & 'Large Point'
J. sambac	'Sujumalige' (single), 'Gundumalli' (double), 'Virupakshi', 'Iravantige', 'Khoya', 'Japani Rai' & 'Motia'

J. trifoliatum	'Grand Duke of Tascany' & 'Floreplano'
P. tuberosa	'Calcutta single', 'Single Mexican', 'Bombay Single', 'Calcutta double', 'Coimbatore Single', 'Bangalore', 'Pantnagar' & 'Double Pearl'
L. odoratus (Sweet Pea)	'Dwarf Cupid', ' Little sweet heart', 'Giant ruffled', 'Kneetti & Cupid ultra dwarf'
N. alata (Nicotiana)	'Sensation Mixed', 'Lime green' & 'Nicki hybrids'
C. moschata (Sweet Sultan)	'Giant Mauve', 'Giant White' & 'Giant Yellow'
D. caryophyllus (Carnation)	'Improved Marguerite' & 'Giant-flowered', 'Chabaud'

C. Research Institutes and Government Departments concerned with the Development of Perfumery and Cut-Flower Trade

1) National Research Development Corporation of India, 61, Ring Rd. Lajpat Nagar III, New Delhi-110024
2) National Botanical Research Institute, Lucknow, Pin 226001
3) Medicinal and Aromatic Plants Divn.
   National Bureau of Plant Genetic Resources
   IARI Campus, New Delhi-110012
4) Central Institute of Medicinal and Aromatic Plants, P.O. Dairy Farm, Nagla, Pin 263149
5) Technical Information Service Division, Publication & Information Directorate C.S.I.R. Hillside Rd., New Delhi-110012
6) Department of Floriculture, Faculty of Horticulture Tamil Nadu Agricultural University, Coimbatore, 641003
7) Project Co-ordinator—Medicinal and Aromatic Plants, National Bureau of Plant Genetic Resources (IARI Campus, New Delhi-110012)

8) Central Horticultural Experiment Station, Ranchi
9) Regional Research Laboratory, Jammu-Tawi
10) Regional Research Laboratory, Bhubaneswar
11) Hindustan Lever Research Station, Andhery (East), Bombay-93

D. Perfume Chemicals contained in Different Flowers

Citrus aurantium	Terpenes, Linalol, Geraniol and Nerol, Methyl anthranilate, Neryl and Geranyl acetates, Linalyl acetate, Nerolidol, Terpineol etc.
Jasminum grandiflorum	Benzyl acelate, Linalyl acetate, Benzyl alcohol, Geraniol, Nerol, Terpineol, Linalol etc.
Michelia champaca	Cineole, Eugenol, Benzyl dehydephenol ethyl alcohol and Methyl anthranilate
Pandanus odoratissimus	Phenylethyl alcohol, Dipentene, Linalol, Phenylethyl acetate, citral etc.
Rose	Citronellol, Geraniol, Nerol, Phenylethyl alcohol, Esters of Geraniol, Eugenol etc.
Tuberose	Geraniol and Nerol, Farnesol, Benzyl alcohol, Benzyl benzoate, Methyl salicylate, Methyl anthranilate, Eugenol and Butyric acid

E. Bibliography

Medicinal and Aromatic Plants Abstract (Publication and Information Directorate, Hillside Road, New Delhi, 110012)

Appropriate Technology, Documentation Bulletin Vol. III No. 6, 1977 (Small Industries Extension Training Institute, Hyderabad-45)

Aromatic Chemicals and Perfumery Industries—Gupta and Dhingra (Delhi Small Business Publication)

Seasonal flowers (Indian summer resources of Mussourie hills) — Navyug Traders 1967

Economic Botany — Biswanathan, 1967

Economic Botany — A. Hill (Tata McGraw Hill, 1972)

Essential Oils and Aromatic Chemicals (New Delhi, SIRI 1980)

Perfume Flavour and Essential Oil Industry — Srivastava (SIRI 1980)

Perfumed Garden of Seikh Nafzaouri—Richard Burton (Arnold Heinemann, 1977)

Fragrant Valley—V. Ramamurthy (Hippie Book Institute, Kurukshetra 1969)

Rose Growing Centres and Rose Industries in India—K. Biswas and V. Narayanaswami (CSIR, 1957)

The Essential Oils (Vols. 1-5) — Ernest Guenther (Van Nostrand Reinhold Co.)

Perfume Cosmetics and Soaps (Vols. 1-3) — W.A. Poucher (Chapman & Hall Ltd.)

Chemistry of Essential Oils and Artificial Perfumes — Parry (Vols. 1-2) (Scott, Greenwood & Sons Ltd., London, 1921-22)

Natural Perfume Materials—Naves & Mazuyer 1947 (Reinhold Publishing Co.)

Ferminger's Manual of Gardening for India—T.A. Ferminger, 1947 (Thacker Spink & Co.)

Development of Essential Oil Industry in U.P.—D.R. Dhingra

The Practice of Modern Perfumery—Krajkeman (Translation) 1954 (Inter Science Publication, New York)

Fragrant Gardens—K.N. Sanecki-Batsford, London

Synthetic Perfumes — T.F. West and others (Edward Arnold, London)

Wealth of India, Vols. V & VII, Parts III & VI (CSIR, New Delhi-12)

Some Beautiful Indian Climbers and Shrubs—The Bombay Natural History Society, 1954

Flowers and Gardens in India — Mrs Templewright (Thacker Spink & Co., 1966)

Floricultural Industry in India—Kolavalli (Oxford IBH, New Delhi)
Perfumery and Essential Oil Records, London
Indian Soap Journal
Directory of Gardening—Chittenden (4 vols.) (Royal Horticultural Society, London)
Sweet Scented Flowers — McDonald, 1895

Articles/Papers

1) Dey, S.C.—Commercial Production of Tuberose Bulbs, 1980
2) Ramkrishna & Kandaswamy—Diseases of Jasmines
3) Krishnaswamy, N.—Flowers, the Exchange Earner
4) Vedamuthu and others—Jasmine Concrete Production
5) Imlappan & Rao—Yield in Edward Rose
6) Imlappan & others—Varietal Evaluation in Tuberose (The above articles appear in the proceedings of the National Seminar on Production Technology for Commercial Flower Crops, 1980—Faculty of Horticulture, Tamil Nadu Agricultural University, Coimbatore-3.)
7) Ranade, G.S.— The Rose Fragrance (Indian Perfumer, Vol. XXIV, No. 2, 1980, pp. 49-56)
8) Muthuswami, S. & others—Production Economics in Jasmine Concrete (Indian Perfumer, Vol. XXIV No. 1, 1980, pp. 43-45)
9) Srivastava, H.C. & Karmarkar, P.G.—An Inventory of Jasmines (Indian Horticulture, Oct-Dec, 1989)
10) Singh & Chatterjee—Tuberose Cultivation in West Bengal (Indian Horticulture Vol. 26, No. 1, April-June, 81)
11) Swaminathan and others—Pilot Plant for Extraction of Jasmine Essential Oil (Indian Horticulture, Vol. 24, No. 1, April-June, 1979)
12) Sambandamurthi & Appavu—Effect of the Chemicals on colouring of Tuberose, 1980
13) Malik, R.S.—Studies in Production of Rose for cut flower (Indian Horticulture, 1980)

F. Dealers of Machineries and Accessories

1) L.C.T. Industries, Trichy Road, Coimbatore-18
2) Teblit Industries, Trichy Road, Coimbatore-18
3) Kamrup Essential Oils, K.R. Choudhury Rd. Bharalumukh, Gauhati, Pin 781 009
4) Kanauj Scent Factories, Kanauj, U.P.
5) Golden Sun Manufacturing Co., Ranvir Building, 70, Princep Street, Bombay-2
6) Bush Boake Allen (India) Ltd. Madras-10
7) Consolidated Solvents & Chemical Corporation 52/58, Babu Genu Road, New Hanuman Lane, Jivraj Shamiji Bldg. 1st floor, Bombay-2
8) Capco Pvt. Ltd., Co-operative Insurance Building, Sir P.M. Road, Bombay-1

G. Manufacturers and Dealers of Essential Oils and Aromatic Chemicals

1) Mysore Sales International Ltd. 5th floor, Shantiniketan, 8, Camac Street, Calcutta-16
2) Government Sandalwood Oil Factory Post Box 6, Shimoga, Karnatak, Pin 577 201
3) Calcutta Essence Supply Co. 41 Ezra Street, Calcutta- 700001
4) Hindustan Sandalwood & Essential Oil Distillers, Kanauj (U.P.)
5) Munkalal Sons & Co., Hina Building, Kanauj (U.P.)
6) Devi Industries, 19, Azad Street, Gandhinagar, Madras-20
7) Ram Krishna Gupta & Brothers, 33/107, Gaya Prasad Lane, Kanpur-1
8) Ghosh Brothers (Perfumers), 50 Ezra Street Calcutta-1
9) Vinode Kumar Rakesh & Co. 74, Mount Rd. Coonoor, Tamil Nadu, 643102
10) Pragdutt & Co., Kanauj (U.P.)
11) Saren Brothers, Kanauj-25 (U.P.)
12) Ram Narayan Pratap Narayan, Kanauj (U.P.)
13) Kanauj Scent Factory, Kanauj (U.P.)

14) Asian Chemical Works, 124-126, S. Gandhi Marg, Bombay-2
15) Bipin Chemicals, 1st Floor, Kanaga Mansion, 660, Kapasia Bazar, Ahmedabad-2
16) Bhausali Chemicals, 11, Ekambareswar, Agraharam, Madras-3
17) Aromatic Products and Chemicals Pvt. Ltd. 42, Prospect Chambers, Annexe, Dadabhai Nauroji Rd. Bombay-1

H. Nurseries dealing in Planting Materials of Fragrant Flowers

1) The Agri-Horticultural Society, 18, Cathedral Road, Madras, 600086
2) Model Nursery, 5/1 Tiljala Road, Calcutta 700046
3) Model Nursery, Mechagram, P.O. Panskura, Midnapore, 721152
4) Shanti Kunj Nursery, B.L. Dikshit Road, Kalimpong, Pin 734301
5) Universal Bulb & Plant Nursery Lower Briddle Rd, Kalimpong 734301
6) Agri-Horticultural Society of India 1, Alipur Rd, Calcutta 700027
7) Imperial Nursery, 9, Rai Charan Pal Lane Tiljala, Calcutta, 700046
8) Edward Nursery, P.O. Botanical Garden, Andul Rd. Howrah, 711101
9) Horticultural Arena, Kadamkanan, Jhargram, Midnapore, Pin 721507 (Author's Nursery)
10) Pratap Nursery, Prem Nagar, Panditwari Dehra Dun (U.P.) Pin 248001
11) L.R. Brothers (Nursery), Venus Cinema Building, Saharanpur, Pin 247001
12) Laveena Roses, 18, Mal Rd., Meerut Cantt. Meerut
13) Kumaon Nursery, Ramnagar, Nainital, Pin 244715
14) Krishi Farm, Natungram, Purba Bidyadharpur, 24 Parganas (N), West Bengal

15) Chandra Nursery, Rhenock, Sikkim, Pin 737133
16) Anand Nursery, Gandhi Nagar, Jaipur, 302015
17) Government Nursery, Dept of Horticulture, Bhubaneswar, Pin 751001
18) K.S.G.'s Farm & Nursery, Sriniwasa, 237/46, 5th Main Road, Chamarajpeth, Bangalore 560018

I. Other Essential Oils

These however are not obtained from flowers. They are extracted from the different plant parts other than flowers. Chiefly they are used for absorbing water-soluble flower perfume in the process of making floral attar. They also find their uses in flower perfume as adulterants.

Sandalwood oil: The plants of santalaceae family yield sandalwood oil through distillation. The plants grow abundantly in western Australia and peninsular India as a forest crop. From Australia the wood is exported to China in plenty. It is a valuable scented ingredient of the soap industry. Its present market price being Rs. 1500-2000 per kilogram. In a high-grade oil the sesquiterpene alcohol content is high. If quality timber is processed through an improved distillation process a good quality oil is produced, which contains as much as 90% of sesquiterpene alcohol.

Palmarosa oil: It is obtained from a grass named *Cymbopogon martini* in this country. An important oil distillation centre being Ilichpur in the district of Amarabati. It is also produced in Berar and Khandesh in lesser quantities. A high-grade oil can be obtained if plants are used just before its flowering in September and October. Maharashtra being the largest producer of Palmarosa oil in India.

The scent of palmarosa oil to some extent is similar to that of rose oil. Hence its extensive use in making spurious rose oil. Once it was used in adulterating rose otto in Bulgaria. Before using as an adulterant its colour and texture (viscosity) are made to appear as that of rose otto. For this purpose some quantity of gum arabic is mixed with palmarosa oil and heated in the sun until the mix looks like rose otto.

Vetiver oil: It is deep brown in colour. Its scent is long lasting, hence valuable in the perfume industry. In many parts of India it (*Vetiveria zizanioides*) is known as *Khas-khas*. Its root is used in making aromatic mats for doors and windows in summer. The plant is cultivated in Rajasthan, Madhya Pradesh, Punjab and the east coast for extracting essential oil and making mats. In Tuticorin and Bharatpur vetiver is grown extensively. Its roots contain aromatic oil. Oil is extracted through distillation. Its dry roots yield 0.2 per cent of oil. For absorbing flower perfume vetiver oil, like sandalwood oil, is kept in the receiver of a distillation plant.

White oil: It is also known as 'liquid paraffin' or 'petroleum jelly'. In preparing balm and cosmetics it is used as a greasy base. White oil is obtained from crude petroleum through fractional distillation. It is suitable for various uses because of its viscosity which varies from that of kerosene oil to jelly-like paraffin. Deodorised kerosene oil can well be used as white oil.

The base-ingredient of chief handkerchief perfumes of the market is white oil. A few drops of otto are mixed with a bottle of white oil.

Citronella oil: It is extracted from a grass named *Cymbopogon nardus*. The oil imported from Java is strongly scented. But the oil of Sri Lanka is sub-standard due to adulteration. Nowadays it is distilled in many parts of India.

A six-month-old crop (grass) is mowed for distillation. Then at an interval of four months the crop is harvested subsequently. It, like vetiver, does not yield quality oil if harvested after flowering. One plantation lasts for five years for a good production of oil. In Java around 15000 acres are under its cultivation. An average oil production per acre is 25 kilo of oil. In making scented soaps citronella oil is used extensively.

Eucalyptus oil: It is distilled from the green leaves of Eucalyptus. The leaves of *E. globulus* are used more for this purpose. This species grows widely in Australia, Tasmania and Algeria. In Australia it is known as 'Blue gum'.

The dry leaves yield about 3% of oil. The oil obtained through distillation is purified by adding alkali. The oil if not purified causes coughing. It is widely used in toothpaste, medicine and soaps.

Agar oil: It is distilled from Agarwood (*Aquilaria malaccensis*). The oil distilled from fungus-infected wood is used in perfumery and medicine. Partially exhausted wood chips are used in *Agarbattis*. Agar oil is a valuable perfume fixative. The wood is graded for its different uses. A grade known as *Dhum* is used for extraction of agar oil. While other grades are mainly for manufacturing incense. Agar oil is stimulant, carminative and astringent. Hence its use in medicine. Agar oil finds its extensive demand in Arabian countries. The popular perfume 'AGURU' is said to be produced from agar oil. This species of *Agar* is Malayan. It has another species, *A. agalocha*.

Index (Species & Cultivars)

Index (General)